Series / Number 07-043

D1245385

BAYESIAN STATISTICAL INFERENCE

GUDMUND R. IVERSEN
Swarthmore College

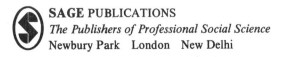

SAGE PUBLICATIONS
The Publishers of Professional Social Science
Newbury Park   London   New Delhi

For information address:

SAGE Publications, Inc.
2111 West Hillcrest Drive
Newbury Park, California 91320

SAGE Publications Ltd.
28 Banner Street
London EC1Y 8QE
England

SAGE Publications India Pvt. Ltd.
M-32 Market
Greater Kailash I
New Delhi 110 048 India

International Standard Book Number 0-8039-2328-7

Library of Congress Catalog Card No. 84-050890

THIRD PRINTING, 1989

When citing a professional paper, please use the proper form. Remember to cite the
correct Sage University Paper series title and include the paper number. One of the
following formats can be adapted (depending on the style manual used):

(1) IVERSEN, GUDMUND R. and NORPOTH, HELMUT (1976) "Analysis of
Variance." Sage University Paper series on Quantitative Applications in the Social
Sciences, 07-001. Beverly Hills and London: Sage Pubns.

OR

(2) Iversen, Gudmund R. and Norpoth, Helmut. 1976. *Analysis of Variance.* Sage
University Paper series on Quantitative Applications in the Social Sciences, series no.
07-001. Beverly Hills and London: Sage Pubns.

CONTENTS

Series Editor's Introduction

Earlier in this series of monographs, we published a paper on tests of significance, which deals with classical inferential statistics. Professor Iversen's paper on Bayesian inference presents an alternative view, one based on the use of prior probabilities in producing posterior probabilities. In the first four chapters, Professor Iversen provides a gentle and lucid introduction to Bayesian methods, and uses several simple examples to ensure comprehension by the neophyte.

Before reading this paper, the reader should have some familiarity with classical statistical inference, particularly elementary probability theory and the binomial distribution. The novice should be prepared to work through carefully, both conceptually and computationally, the materials and examples presented in Chapter 5. If he or she is willing to make that investment, then Chapters 6-8 will be more meaningful, and the novice may consider himself or herself more than a novice once the entire manuscript is digested.

Professor Iversen covers the use of Bayes' theorem and statistical inference in estimating various parameters, including proportions, means, correlations, regression, and variances. In each instance he compares classical methods of inference with Bayesian methods, and in the latter chapters he delineates the strengths and weaknesses of Bayesian inference, ultimately making the argument that these methods are to be preferred to classical ones. Whether or not the introductory reader is convinced by these arguments, he or she will certainly have a greater understanding of what Bayesian statistics involves, and of its advantages and disadvantages, after studying this monograph carefully.

Iversen is particularly careful to point out that one of the major criticisms of Bayesian statistics—the subjective nature of the prior probabilities—applies with equal force in classical inferential theory, with regard to selecting confidence levels for hypothesis testing. Another strong point is Iversen's treatment of the relative impact of prior distributions, and of information gained from the actual data, on posterior probabilities. He examines the sensitivity of both of these components under varying conditions, and thereby gives the novice a good sense of the relative contribution of subjective assumptions about prior information versus the data collected for the study under analysis. Other discoveries likely to interest the beginning reader include the fact that classical statistical methods provide the same numerical results, in terms of confidence intervals, as do Bayesian methods that assume uniform prior distributions; however, the interpretations of these results will differ, and so the researcher may calculate such results using conventional methods but provide a Bayesian interpretation for them, should such a prior distribution make sense. The reader is likely to find some considerable intuitive appeal to Bayesian methods, and to realize its broad range of application in each of the various social science disciplines.

-John L. Sullivan
Series Co-Editor

BAYESIAN STATISTICAL INFERENCE

GUDMUND R. IVERSEN
Swarthmore College

1. THOMAS BAYES AND STATISTICAL INFERENCE

Bayesian statistics provides an alternative to hypothesis testing and confidence interval estimation. It takes its name from the English clergyman Thomas Bayes, who died in 1760. A paper by Bayes (1763) contains a version of an equality among several probabilities that today is known as Bayes' theorem. When the paper was first published there was little reason to expect that this rather simple equality would be used for anything more than the solution of certain problems in probability theory. But two hundred years later Bayes' theorem has taken on a new importance and now provides the foundation for Bayesian statistical inference.

Statistical inference is used to draw conclusions from the known data in our samples to populations for which we do not have data. For example, we know that 55 percent of the voters in our sample intend to vote a certain way, but how many intend to vote that way in the population of all voters? One way to make a statement about the population percentage would be to set up a null hypothesis that the population percentage equals, say 50 percent, and use the sample data for the test of whether this hypothesis could be rejected or not. A related procedure would be to use the sample data and estimate the unknown

AUTHOR'S NOTE: *The manuscript benefited from comments by Bobbie Iversen and two referees and from word processing beyond the call of duty by Naomi Marcus. I am grateful to Larry Ehmer for the graphs in Chapter 4, and the data for the example on the mean in Chapter 5 were made available by the Inter-university Consortium for Political and Social Research. The data for the Quality of American Life, 1978, were originally collected by the Center for Political Studies of the Institute for Social Research, the University of Michigan, under a grant from the National Science Foundation. Neither the original collectors of the data nor the Consortium bears any responsibility for the analyses or the interpretations presented here.*

7

population percentage by a confidence interval. Alternatively, we could use Bayesian statistics to make statements about the population percentage.

Statistical inference, no matter how it is done, involves an extrapolation from the known sample to the larger and unknown population. Because we are extrapolating, we can never be certain our conclusions are correct. This uncertainty is dealt with using probabilities, whether they are called significance level, confidence level, or Bayesian prior and posterior probabilities.

The choice of which way we do statistical inference rests in a very fundamental way with how we define the concept of probability. The mathematical theory of probability is not very concerned with how probabilities are measured, but if we are to use probabilities we have to have some way of assigning numerical values to them. The choice between doing statistical inference using hypothesis testing and confidence interval estimation (known as classical statistical inference) and Bayesian statistics depends on how we measure probabilities. The two types of probabilities relevant here can be called empirical and subjective probabilities. A third type of probability is the necessary, or logical concept of probability. It is not discussed here, and for a presentation of this view see Barnett (1982).

The empirical view sees probabilities as long-run relative frequencies or proportions, and some people therefore call them frequentist probabilities or objective probabilities. Imagine that an experiment is repeated many times, and each time one of several events occurs. As the number of times the experiment is done gets larger, the proportion of times a particular event occurs approaches the probability of that event. For example, let the experiment consist of tossing a die, and this experiment is repeated a large number of times. The event that 1 or 2 comes up occurs one-third of the time, and this leads us to say that the probability of 1 or 2 equals one-third. This view was first formulated by Venn (1886) and later led to the Neyman-Pearson system of classical statistical inference with hypothesis testing and confidence interval estimation.

The significance level for the test of a statistical null hypothesis is an example of such a relative frequency. If the null hypothesis is true and we drew many different samples from the same population, the sample test statistics will still fall in the rejection region of the test for some of the samples. Those are the samples for which we will erroneously reject the null hypothesis, and the long-run proportion of times this will happen is the significance level of the test. For a critical examination of some of the issues relevant to this type of statistical inference, see Chapter 2.

The subjective view takes probabilities as personal measures of uncertainty, based on the available evidence. Since our available evidence is mostly empirical, both views often come up with the same numerical value for a particular probability. The subjectivist would also say that the probability equals one-third that a fair die comes up 1 or 2 when tossed because of what is known about the physics of dice tossing, the even distribution of mass in the die and because from past tosses the proportion of 1 and 2 is one-third.

But, with subjective probabilities we can also use probabilities on events that cannot be repeated. A political scientist can express the probability that a first-term president will run for election again based on the current political climate, what the president has said about running again, and the like. We cannot watch this president several times, rolling back time and counting the proportion of times the president decided to run again. Thus, there is no empirical, experimental basis for the probability that the president will run again, and anyone using classical statistical inference cannot consider the possibility of a second campaign in probabilistic terms. Subjective probabilities are more general than empirical probabilities since they can also be used to measure the uncertainty we have about single, unique events. At the same time, they are not unique. Since two reasonable people may have different information available to them about the president's intention, their subjective probabilities may well differ on the question of whether the president will run for a second term.

The path-breaking work on subjective probabilities was done by Ramsey (1926), followed by deFinetti in the 1930s and Savage (1954). For a discussion of the subjective view of probability, including deFinetti's best-known paper, see Kyburg and Smokler (1980), deFinetti (1982), and Jeffrey (1983).

2. CLASSICAL STATISTICAL INFERENCE

Almost all statistical inference performed in the social sciences today makes use of hypothesis testing of one form or another. For a presentation of this view see Henkel (1976). But, in spite of its popularity, there are drawbacks to classical statistical inference, which can be remedied by Bayesian methods. In order to motivate and provide a better understanding of Bayesian statistics, we take a critical look at certain features of classical methods. The presentation of Bayes' theorem and Bayesian statistics continues in Chapter 3. For a discussion of different methods of statistical inference see Barnett (1982).

Use of Tail Probabilities

Suppose we want to study whether a population is evenly divided between men and women. The statistical null hypothesis is that the probability equals 0.5 that a randomly chosen person is female. We will draw a random sample of 10 people, and we will make it a two-sided test. If the null hypothesis is true, the binomial distribution can be used to find that the probability of the sample's containing 0 women (and 10 men) equals 1/1024. Similarly, the probability of 1 woman (and 9 men) equals 10/1024, the probability of 9 women (and 1 man) equals 10/1024, and the probability that all 10 people are women equals 1/1024. If we reject the null hypothesis for 0, 1, 9, or 10 women, the significance level of the test equals the sum of these probabilities, 22/1024 = 0.02.

The sample can now be drawn, and suppose there are 9 women among the 10 people. Because the result falls in the rejection region for this test, we can report that the null hypothesis is rejected with a 0.02 significance level. This significance level consists partly of the probability of the observed data, and it seems quite reasonable that the evidence in the sample data should be used in the decision about the null hypothesis. But the significance level also contains the probabilities for 0, 1, or 10 women, and these are data that did not occur. Thus, in classical statistics we are in the strange situation that probabilities of various data that *did not occur* are used as evidence against the null hypothesis.

The reason users of classical statistical inference get into this difficulty is that the theory is based on probabilities as long run relative frequencies. The significance level tells us what will happen in the long run, if we draw a large number of samples. With a true null hypothesis we will find that 2 percent of the samples fall in the rejection region and lead to an erroneous rejection of the hypothesis. Thus, before the data are collected the significance level, as a probability, is a very meaningful quantity. But we do not have many samples; we have only one sample.

After that sample is known, it becomes more difficult to interpret the significance level relative to the one sample.

Interpretation of Confidence Intervals

The same difficulty with the use of probabilities after the sample data are known is found in the interpretation of confidence intervals. The theory states that in the long run with data from many samples and therefore many confidence intervals, a certain proportion of these intervals will contain the true parameter value while the remaining intervals will not. Thus, the theory predicts what will happen in the long run, before any data are collected. The difficulty arises with what to do with the probabilities after the data from our one sample are known. The one confidence interval from our sample either contains or does not contain the true parameter, only we do not know whether our one interval belongs to the large set of intervals that do contain the parameter or to the small set of intervals that do not contain the parameter. All we can do is hope that our single, known interval belongs to the first set.

Uncertainty about Parameter Values

This discussion of tail probabilities and confidence intervals points to the fact that classical statistical inference does not address the question we really want to have answered. The purpose of statistical inference is to learn something about the unknown values of population parameters. We are uncertain about the parameter values, and in order to learn about the parameters we collect sample data. As long as we have only sample data, we cannot hope to find the exact values of the paramenters, but we know more after the sample data have been studied than we did before. Thus, we are uncertain about the paramenter values before the sample data are collected, but the new evidence contained in the sample will tell us something about the parameter values. Even after this information in the sample is known to us we will be uncertain about the parameter values, but our uncertainty will have been reduced. What we need is a method of statistical inference that starts with our initial uncertainty about the parameter values and then modifies this uncertainty by using the information contained in the sample.

For a more extensive discussion of classical statistics as seen by Bayesian statisticians, see Berger (1980), Edwards et al. (1963), and Rosenkrantz (1977).

3. BAYES' THEOREM

Derivation

The formal derivation of the equality among certain probabilities known as Bayes' theorem is based on the fact that the joint probability of two events P and D can be written as the product of the probability of one of the events and conditional probability of the second event, given the first event. In symbols this can be written in the equation

$$Prob(PD) = Prob(P) \cdot Prob(D|P) \qquad [1]$$

By reversing the two events the joint probability of the two events can also be written

$$Prob(DP) = Prob(D) \cdot Prob(P|D) \qquad [2]$$

Since the two left sides are equal, it follows that the two right sides are equal. Equating the right sides and rearranging we get

$$Prob(P|D) = \frac{Prob(D|P) \circ Prob(P)}{Prob(D)} \qquad [3]$$

Finally, it may be that there are several different P's, namely P1, P2, .., Pk, which are exclusive and exhaustive. In that case, the probability of D in the denominator can be written as a weighted sum of the conditional probabilities Prob(D|Pi) where the weights are Prob(Pi).

For the event Pi, the equation above becomes

$$Prob(Pi|D) = \frac{Prob(D|Pi)Prob(Pi)}{Prob(D|P1)Prob(P1) + \ldots + Prob(D|Pk)Prob(Pk)} \qquad [4]$$

This is Bayes' theorem for the discrete case with k different P's.

The particular letters P and D were chosen for a purpose, P standing for population and D for data. The left side of Bayes' theorem then becomes the probability that we are dealing with the ith population Pi, given the observed data D. The probability Prob(D|Pi) represents the probability of the observed data D, given that it comes from population Pi. Finally, Prob(Pi) is the probability that we are dealing with the population Pi before any data are known to us. The end of the analysis is the probability on the left side of the equal sign, and it is found from the probabilities on the right side of the equal sign.

An Example

We have three different communities, which can be thought of as populations P1, P2, and P3, and we want to know from which of these populations our sample data come. In P1, 30 percent of the people are Catholic, in P2, 50 percent are Catholic, and in P3, 70 percent are Catholic. We will choose one of these communities at random by tossing a die and use P1 if the die comes up 1 or 2, P2 if the die comes up 3 or 4, and P3 if it comes up 5 or 6. From the chosen community we will select a random sample of one person. Suppose this person is Catholic, which means that our data D consist of one Catholic in a sample of one. We do not know which community was chosen; all we know are the data. We are therefore interested in the probabilities that this person came from each of the three communities P1, P2, and P3.

Since the initial choice of community was made at random with equal probabilities, each community had a probability of one-third of being chosen. Thus, Prob(P1) = Prob(P2) = Prob(P3) = 0.333. These are the so-called *prior probabilities*, since they give the probabilities of the three populations before the data are known.

The other probabilities we need to know in order to use Bayes' theorem are the three data probabilities Prob(D|P1), Prob(D|P2) and Prob(D|P3). If the person came from P1, where there are 30 percent Catholics, the data probability Prob(Catholic|Community 1) equals 0.3. If the person were sampled from the second community with 50 percent Catholics, the data probability equals 0.5, and, similarly, the probability that a randomly drawn person from the third community is Catholic equals 0.7, since 70 percent of that population is Catholic. Thus, the three data probabilities are

$$\text{Prob}(D|P1) = 0.3$$
$$\text{Prob}(D|P2) = 0.5$$
$$\text{Prob}(D|P3) = 0.7$$

According to Bayes' theorem we now get

$$\text{Prob}(P1|D) = \frac{0.3(0.333)}{0.3(0.333) + 0.5(0.333) + 0.7(0.333)} = \frac{0.0999}{0.4995} = 0.20$$

$$\text{Prob}(P2 \mid D) = \frac{0.5(0.333)}{0.3(0.333) + 0.5(0.333) + 0.7(0.333)} = \frac{0.1665}{0.4995} = 0.33$$

$$\text{Prob}(P3 \mid D) = \frac{0.7(0.333)}{0.3(0.333) + 0.5(0.333) + 0.7(0.333)} = \frac{0.2331}{0.4995} = 0.47$$

These are the *posterior* probabilities. They tell us that after we know the data consist of a sample of one person who is Catholic, the probability equals 0.20 that the data came from P1, 0.33 that it came from P2, and 0.47 that is came from P3. Before we knew the data each community had a probability of 0.33, and knowledge of the data changed two of the probabilities. The knowledge that the sample data consisted of a Catholic makes it more than twice as likely that the data came from the third rather than the first population, and the third population is about 50 percent more likely than the second population.

Computations like these can conveniently be arranged in a table as shown in Table 1. The first column identifies the populations, and the second column gives the value of the population parameter, in this case the percentage of Catholics. The third column gives the prior probabilities of the various population parameters, and the numbers in this column always add up to 1.00. The fourth column gives the probabilities of the observed data, depending on which of the populations the data come from. The fifth column gives the product of the data probability and the prior probability for each of the populations. Each of these three products is the numerator in Bayes' theorem for the various populations, and the sum of the products is the denominator. Finally, the last column gives the posterior probabilities, obtained by dividing each product in the previous column by the sum of the products.

Let us carry this example one step further and collect some more data. At this stage our uncertainty about which population is producing our data is reflected in the three probabilities 0.20, 0.33, and 0.47. Most likely the third population is the source of the data, but the probabilities for the other two populations are large enough that those populations cannot be ruled out. The only way to get a better sense of which of the three populations we are dealing with is to gather more information.

The new data consist of an additional sample from the same, but to us unknown, population as before. There are 10 people in the new sample, and 8 of them are Catholics. The prior probabilities for the three populations are the old posterior probabilities 0.20, 0.33, and 0.47. The data probabilities are found by using the binomial distribution. If these

TABLE 1
Example of Computation for Bayes' Theorem

Population	Percentage Catholics	Prior Probabilities	Data Probabilities	Product	Posterior Probabilities
P		Prob (Pi)	Prob (D|Pi)	Prob (D/Pi) Prob (Pi)	Prob (Pi|D)
(1)	(2)	(3)	(4)	(5) = (4) (3)	(6)
1	30	0.333	0.3	0.0999	0.20
2	50	0.333	0.5	0.1665	0.33
3	70	0.333	0.7	0.2331	0.47
		Sum 0.999		Sum 0.4995 = P(D)	Sum 1.00

data come from the first population where there are 30 percent Catholics, the probability of 8 Catholics and 2 non-Catholics in a sample of 10 becomes

$$\text{Prob}(\text{Data}\,|\,P1) = \begin{bmatrix} 10 \\ 8 \end{bmatrix} 0.3^8 (1 - 0.3)^2 = 0.00145 \qquad [5]$$

Similarly, if these data come from the second population, the data probability becomes

$$\text{Prob}(\text{Data}\,|\,P2) = \begin{bmatrix} 10 \\ 8 \end{bmatrix} 0.5^8 (1 - 0.5)^2 = 0.04394 \qquad [6]$$

If the data come from the third population,

$$\text{Prob}(\text{Data}\,|\,P3) = \begin{bmatrix} 10 \\ 8 \end{bmatrix} 0.7^8 (1 - 0.7)^2 = 0.23347 \qquad [7]$$

The data probabilities are then combined with the prior probabilities in Bayes' theorem to produce the posterior probabilities. Numerically the posterior probabilities become

$$\text{Prob}(P1\,|\,\text{Data}) = 0.002$$
$$\text{Prob}(P2\,|\,\text{Data}) = 0.115$$
$$\text{Prob}(P3\,|\,\text{Data}) = 0.883$$

From these posterior probabilities we see that our uncertainty about which of the three populations generated the data has changed considerably. It is almost impossible that the data could have come from the first population P1. Most likely these data come from P3.

Bayesian analysis is cumulative. In the example above, the original prior distribution was first modified by the information from the sample of one observation. The resulting posterior distribution was then used as the prior distribution in the next analysis, where we brought in the information from the second sample of 10 people. We would have gotten the same final posterior distribution if we had started with the original prior distribution and used as our sample the information that in a sample of 11 there were 9 Catholics.

One Population

We are now told that there are not three different populations out there; it is really only one population. But it is known that the percentage of Catholics in this population is either 30, 50, or 70. How is this situation different from what we have done earlier? When there actually were three populations to choose from and we used the toss of a die to decide from which population the data would be drawn, then there were three actual, true values of the population percentage Catholics and each population had an equal chance of being used. Now there is only one population and one actual, true percentage of Catholics. But we are still as uncertain about whether the true percentage is 30, 50, or 70 when there is one population as when there are three populations. Since we could use Bayesian analysis in the case of three populations, we should also be able to use it in the case of one population.

The major difference lies in the nature of the prior distribution. In the first case we could toss a die and from this process determine directly that each population had a probability of one-third of being used as the source of the data. Now we only have one population, and there is no mechanism like the toss of a die to determine the prior probability that the percentage of Catholics is 30, 50, or 70. However, if probability is a personal measure of uncertainty, what we need to do is express our uncertainties about the three possible percentages in three probabilities that add up to 1.00. Our Bayesian analyst may not know much about this particular population and on this basis concludes that the three percentages are equally likely. This translates directly into probabilities of one-third as the prior probabilities for the three possible percentages.

There is nothing right or wrong about these prior probabilities. Both you and I may prefer different sets of three probabilities, based on what each of us knows about religious preferences in this population. Prior probabilities are personal measures of uncertainty, and they may well differ from one person to the next. The effects of differing prior distributions are discussed further in Chapter 6 (on prior distributions).

Going back to equal prior probabilities of one-third for each of the three possible percentages, the remaining part of the Bayesian analysis is identical to the analysis we have already done. After finding 9 Catholics among 11 people in our data, the posterior probabilities are

$$\text{Prob}(30\% | \text{Data}) = 0.002$$
$$\text{Prob}(50\% | \text{Data}) = 0.115$$
$$\text{Prob}(70\% | \text{Data}) = 0.883$$

Since we are no longer dealing with three different populations, each with its own percentage of Catholics, but with one population with one unknown percentage of Catholics, we write the posterior probabilities as probabilities of each of the percentages instead of as probabilities of each of the populations.

The data have changed our uncertainties about the unknown percentage of Catholics in this population. From equal probabilities of one-third we now believe that there is only a very small probability of 0.002 that the population is 30 percent Catholic, there is a fairly small probability of 0.115 that the percentage equals 50, and there is an overwhelming probability of 0.883 that the percentage equals 70.

A figure like a population percentage is known as a population parameter, just as other population characteristics (e.g., means, variances, and regression coefficients). Bayesian statistical inference assigns probabilities to the possible parameter values, and through Bayes' theorem these probabilities are updated in light of the evidence contained in the data. In Bayesian analysis the parameter is seen as a variable, with its own probability distribution, since the value of the parameter is unknown. In our earlier example the percentage Catholic is taken as a discrete variable with three possible values, but it is also possible to have parameters as continuous variables. In either case we know that the parameter has one specific, true value. But as long as we are uncertain about what that particular value is, we treat the parameter as a variable and use probabilities to express our uncertainties about the parameter values.

4. BAYESIAN METHODS FOR
A PROPORTION

Bayesian procedures for the study of a variety of population parameters are presented in this chapter and the next. Each procedure requires a prior distribution for the unknown parameter, and this prior distribution must be specified by the researcher. That raises questions about how we find prior distributions and how important they are for the analysis.

Instead of going into these issues here, we present the Bayesian methods first and postpone a more detailed discussion of prior distributions until Chapter 6. (But if a reader wants a better understanding of prior distributions before getting into the specific methods, he or she may read Chapter 6 first.)

Proportion

Sample surveys are often taken in order to estimate what proportion of a population possesses a certain characteristic. Every month the government takes a survey and the resulting percentage of unemployed always makes the headlines. The proportions of viewers watching various television programs set the fees for commercials and determine the profitability of stations and networks. Similarly, the proportions of a population holding views on current issues together determine public opinion, which again influence policymakers.

In each of these examples the data result in an observed sample proportion. Statistical inference is used to draw conclusions about the corresponding unknown population proportion. This chapter presents a Bayesian way of inferring a population proportion from sample data. Because it is the first example of a realistic Bayesian analysis, the presentation is more drawn out and detailed than for the parameters discussed in the next chapter.

Bayesian statistical analysis of a population proportion goes beyond the example in the previous section, where we permit only three values—0.3, 0.5, and 0.7—for the unknown population proportion. Let the unknown population proportion be denoted π. As long as the true, fixed value of π is unknown to us, we consider π to be a variable. Because it can take on any value between 0 and 1, π becomes a continuous variable. This notation using π is not very common for a proportion, but it is consistent with the general rule that the population parameters are denoted by Greek letters.

Bayes' theorem works just as well for continuous variables as for discrete variables. Instead of assigning probabilities to specific values of the variable the way it was done in the example above, we use continuous probability densities for the prior and posterior distributions. The mathematical manipulations may seem difficult, but we do not discuss the general theory. Instead, we do examples and give the results, starting with the population proportion in this chapter.

Just as in the discrete example above, the analysis starts with a prior distribution for the unknown parameter. After specifying the prior distribution the data are collected, and Bayes' theorem is used to combine the prior distribution and the information in the data into the posterior distribution for the parameter.

An example. Continuing with our religious example, let π be the proportion of adults in the population who identify themselves as Catholics. My own knowledge of π is limited, but I am almost certain π is less than 0.5. It is quite likely that π lies somewhere between 0.2 and 0.4, and I would be surprised if π were less than 0.2 or larger than 0.4. Extrapolating from this vague knowledge I am able to draw the density shown in Figure 1.

The graph is drawn in such a way that the total area between the curve and the horizontal axis equals 1.00. This means that the graph displays a probability density, and areas under the curve can be interpreted as probabilities. The graph shows that most of the probability is located between 0.1 and 0.5 and maybe as much as two-thirds of the probability lies between 0.2 and 0.4. Thus, this graph corresponds well to the limited knowledge of π expressed in the previous paragraph.

There is nothing in Bayesian analysis requiring this to be "the correct" prior distribution of the unknown parameter. Quite the contrary, another person analyzing the same problem could well have a different prior distribution, expressing that person's uncertainties about the parameter. The question of whether different prior distributions make any difference for the final conclusions is discussed in Chapter 6.

The next step consists of finding a way to incorporate our prior distribution in Bayes' theorem. Because π is seen as a continuous variable, it has infinitely many possible values between 0 and 1. Therefore, we cannot work with individual values as we did in the first

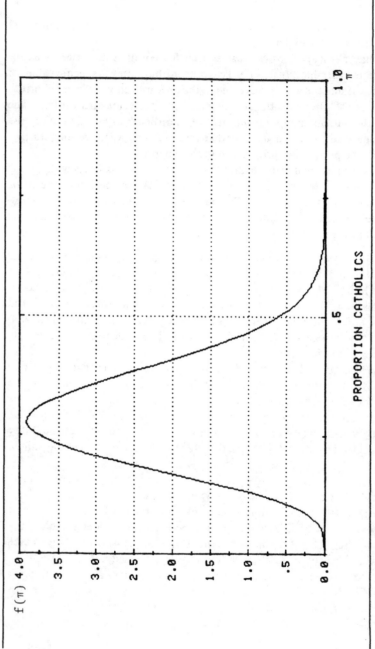

Figure 1: Prior Distribution for π, the Proportion of Catholics in the Adult U.S. Population

example, where it was assumed that there were only 3 possible values of π. One way to deal with a continuous variable is to find the mathematical function for the curve in Figure 1. The actual mathematical function contains the same information as the curve itself, and the function can be used in the continuous version of Bayes' theorem.

Mathematicians have equations for a large variety of curves, and for the analysis of a population proportion it turns out that it is particularly convenient to look at functions that are polynomials in π. Here are some examples of such polynomials:

$$f(\pi) = 2\pi = 2\pi^1(1 - \pi)^0$$
$$f(\pi) = 6\pi - 6\pi^2 = 6\pi^1(1 - \pi)^1$$
$$f(\pi) = 12\pi - 24\pi^2 + 12\pi^3 = 12\pi^1(1 - \pi)^2 \qquad [8]$$

None of these will give the curve in Figure 1 when they are plotted. For example, the first function will give a straight line.

But all three functions are of the same kind, they are all polynomials that can be written as a product of three parts, a numerical constant, π to some exponent, and $1 - \pi$ to some exponent. The purpose of the constant is to adjust the curve in such a way that the area between the curve and the horizontal axis equals 1.00, thereby making the function a probability density. The shape of the curve is adjusted by the exponents for π and $1 - \pi$. When the exponents are larger than zero, the curve starts at the origin and reaches the horizontal axis again for $\pi = 1$, as does the curve in Figure 1. The larger the exponents, the more peaked the curve is. When the exponent for π is larger than the exponent for $1 - \pi$, then the curve peaks for some value of π larger than 0.5. When the exponent for $1 - \pi$ is the larger one, then the curve peaks for some value of less than 0.5. Thus, the mathematical function for the curve in Figure 1 has the exponent for $1 - \pi$ larger than the exponent for π.

The function for the curve in Figure 1 can be written

$$f(\pi) = 162{,}792\pi^5(1 - \pi)^{13}$$
$$= C'\pi^{6-1}(1 - \pi)^{14-1} \qquad [9]$$

The constant term 162,792 is not of much interest, and in the second formulation it is replaced by the letter C'. The exponent for π equals 5 and the exponent for $1 - \pi$ equals 13, and in the second formulation the exponents are written $6 - 1$ and $14 - 1$.

This is because the general formula is often written

$$f(\pi) = C'\pi^{a-1}(1 - \pi)^{b-1} \tag{10}$$

and it is easier to find the numbers a and b first and thereby find a – 1 and b – 1. This last function is the general expression for a probability density known as the *beta* distribution. It is characterized by two non-negative constants a and b, and the values of the variable always range from 0 to 1. When a and b are integers, the constant C' in equation 10 becomes

$$C' = \frac{(a + b - 1)!}{(a - 1)!(b - 1)!} \tag{11}$$

It is important to realize that the beta distribution is very different from the binomial distribution. Even though both distributions have constants that are expressed in terms of factorials, the constant for the beta distribution C' cannot be written as a binomial coefficient. One way to see that is to realize that there are a + b – 1 factors in the numerator for C' and only (a – 1) + (b – 1) = a + b – 2 factors in the denominator, while binomial coefficients have the same number of factors in numerator and denominator. Furthermore, the beta distribution is a distribution for a continuous variable that ranges in value from 0 to 1, and the exponents are constants. In the binomial distribution the variable is found in the exponents, and it is a discrete variable, ranging in value from 0 to n.

There are two major ways we can find our particular beta prior distribution; that is, to find the two constants a and b that determine the distribution. The first way is simply by trial and error, preferably using a computer, plotting beta distributions for various values of a and b and simply picking the one that most closely represents our prior knowledge. Figure 1 shows the curve for the beta distribution with a = 6 and b = 14. The curves for nearby values of a and b would not be very different, and there could well be other curves that represent our limited knowledge equally well.

The second way of finding our prior distribution starts with first specifying the expected value and standard deviation of the random variable π. The expected value of π is the center of gravity of the distribution, and let us agree that the distribution should balance at π =

0.30. Since most of the probability should lie between 0.10 and 0.50, it seems reasonable that there should be two standard deviations from the mean at 0.30 up to 0.50, which is a distance of 0.20. If this is two standard deviations, then one standard deviation equals 0.10.

A property of the beta distribution is that the mean and variance can be found directly from a and b. From this follows that a and b can be found from the mean and variance. Let the mean of π be denoted μ and the standard deviation be denoted σ. When the distribution of π is the beta distribution with parameters a and b, we have the following relationships between the mean and variance and the two constants a and b,

$$\mu = \frac{a}{a+b} \qquad \sigma^2 = \frac{\mu(1-\mu)}{a+b+1} \qquad [12]$$

Solving for a and b gives us a and b as the following functions of the mean and the variance,

$$a = \mu\left[\frac{\mu(1-\mu)}{\sigma^2} - 1\right] \qquad b = \left[1-\mu\right]\left[\frac{\mu(1-\mu)}{\sigma^2} - 1\right] \qquad [13]$$

If we know the mean and variance, these two expressions can be used to find a and b.

Since we have already determined that $\mu = 0.30$ and $\sigma = 0.10$, we get

$$a = 0.3\left[\frac{0.3(1-0.3)}{0.01} - 1\right] = 6$$

$$b = (1-0.3)\left[\frac{0.3(1-0.3)}{0.01} - 1\right] = 14$$

as the values of a and b for our example. These values give the expression in equation 9, and that function is used to draw the curve in Figure 1.

The formulas for a and b are such that after substituting for the mean and variance, the resulting values for a and b are not always integers, as they turned out to be in the example. It is possible to use noninteger values for a and b, but then we have to go from factorials to the mathematical function known as the gamma function. This is almost never worth the extra effort involved, and we usually round off a and b to the nearest integer values if they turn out not to be integers.

The prior distribution is now fully specified, both as a curve and as a mathematical function, and it is time to turn to the other source of information about π, namely the data. The data are obtained from a random sample of 1830 people, 420 of whom identified themselves as Catholics in response to a question of religious affiliation.

Bayes' theorem calls for the probability of getting 420 Catholics and 1410 non-Catholics, given that the population proportion of Catholics equals π. This probability is found by using the binomial distribution, since we are dealing with a dichotomy, constant probability π, and independence between observations. According to the binomial distribution, the probability of these data becomes

$$\text{Prob}(\text{Data} \mid \pi) = \begin{bmatrix} 1830 \\ 420 \end{bmatrix} \pi^{420}(1 - \pi)^{1410} \qquad [14]$$

The parameter π is unknown and we cannot find the numerical value of this data probability, but all the information about π contained in the data is expressed in this probability as it is written in equation 14.

We get the numerator in Bayes' theorem by multiplying the data probability in equation 14 and the prior probability in equation 9,

$$\begin{bmatrix} 1830 \\ 420 \end{bmatrix} \pi^{420}(1-\pi)^{1410} \cdot 162{,}792\pi^{5}(1-\pi)^{13} = C\pi^{425}(1-\pi)^{1423} \qquad [15]$$

where the constant C equals the product of the binomial coefficient and 162,792. The exponent 425 comes from adding 420 and 5, and the exponent 1423 is the sum of 1410 and 13.

In the discrete case discussed earlier, the denominator was a sum of three products of the type shown in the equation above. In the continuous case, like the one we are dealing with here, the denominator is an integral over all values of π from 0 to 1. But, in both cases, the denominator is simply a constant needed to make the total probability under the curve equal 1.0.

Since the denominator is just a constant, whatever it is, it can be combined with the constant in equation 15 into a new constant called C″. That way the posterior distribution for π then becomes

$$f(\pi \,|\, \text{data}) = C''\pi^{425}(1 - \pi)^{1423}$$

$$= C''\pi^{426-1}(1 - \pi)^{1424-1} \qquad [16]$$

The only difference between this expression and the one in equation 9 for the prior distribution for π is that the exponents and the constants have changed. The expression above and the prior distribution have the same form, and this means that the posterior distribution for π is also a beta distribution. Because it is a beta distribution, we know directly from equations 10 and 11 that

$$C'' = \frac{(426 + 1424 - 1)!}{(426 - 1)!(1424 - 1)!} = \frac{1849!}{425!\,1423!}$$

This is a very large number without much interest unless we want to graph the curve of equation 16.

Because the posterior distribution for π is a beta distribution, we know directly from equation 12 that the posterior mean of π equals

$$\text{posterior mean} = \frac{426}{426 + 1424} = \frac{426}{1850} = 0.230$$

and

$$\text{posterior variance} = \frac{0.230(1 - 0.230)}{426 + 1424 + 1} = 0.0000958$$

posterior standard deviation = 0.0098

The graph of the posterior distribution is shown in Figure 2. Most of the total probability is now concentrated between 0.21 and 0.25, and we are therefore almost certain that π lies somewhere between those two values. More specifically, even though the curve in Figure 2 represents a beta distribution, it is symmetric enough to be approximated by a normal distribution. Since the standard deviation of π equals 0.0098, 1.96 standard deviations equals 0.019. Adding and subtracting this number from the mean gives us 0.211 and 0.249, and the probability equals 0.95 that π lies between these two values. Formally, this can be written

$$\text{Prob}(0.211 < \pi < 0.249) = 0.95$$

The probability 0.95 comes from the normal distribution, where the probability equals 0.95 that the standard normal variable Z lies between −1.96 and 1.96.

Our initial uncertainty about π is expressed in the prior distribution in Figure 1. The sample data give us considerably more information about π, and our current uncertainty is expressed in the posterior distribution in Figure 2. A comparison of the two distributions shows the change in uncertainty about π. We used to think that π could be almost anywhere between 0 and 0.60, and now we are 95% certain that it lies between 0.21 and 0.25. The data squeezed the probability mass in Figure 1 into the peaked distribution in Figure 2. The total area under each curve still equals 1.00, but it is difficult to compare the two graphs because the vertical scales are very different. It is easier to compare the two curves when they are drawn to the same scale, as shown in Figure 3.

Both the formula for the posterior mean of π and the curves in Figure 3 help give us an understanding of the effect of the prior distribution. The posterior mean can be written

$$\frac{426}{1850} = \frac{420 + 6}{1830 + 20}$$

$$= \frac{\text{\# Catholics in sample + prior constant } a}{\text{\# observations in sample + prior constants } (a+b)}$$

The estimated value of π from the sample above equals the sample proportion $420/1830 = 0.230$. If we take the posterior mean of π as the estimated value of π from the Bayesian analysis, we see that the numerator is increased by 6 and the denominator is increased by 20 compared to the sample proportion. The effect of the prior distribution can therefore be seen as increasing the sample size by 20, 6 of whom are Catholics. The

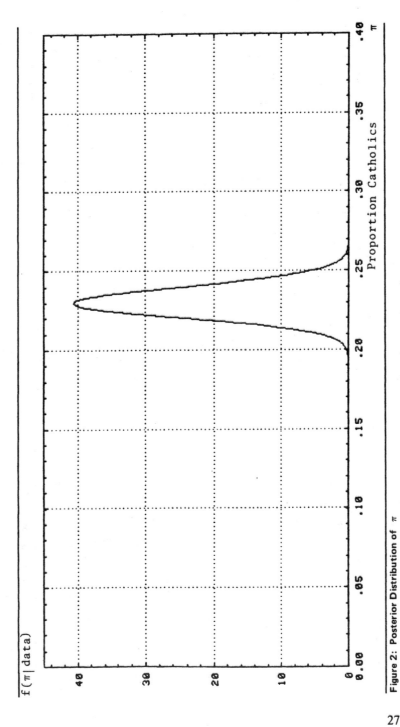

f(π|data)

Figure 2: Posterior Distribution of π

28

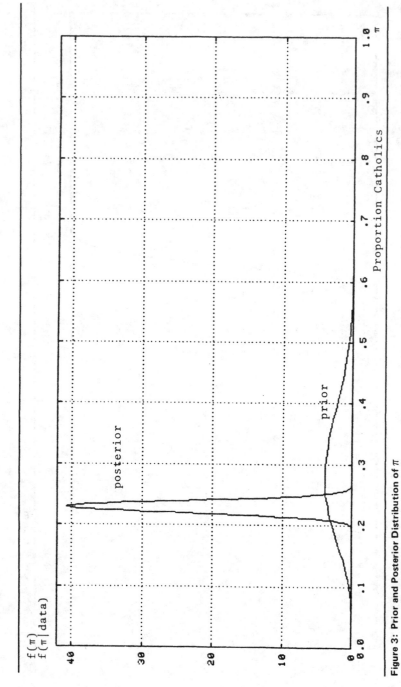

$$f(\pi)$$
$$f(\pi | data)$$

Figure 3: Prior and Posterior Distribution of π

prior knowledge can be said to be worth a sample of 20 observations, and the data are worth a sample of 1850 observations.

This means that here the posterior distribution is heavily determined by the information in the data, and the prior distribution contributed very little. This is not surprising. We did not have much prior knowledge about the proportion of Catholics, and this is the very reason the sample was taken. The sample is quite large, and we learned much from it. This also means that if other people had used different prior distributions, meaning other values of a and b, the posterior distributions would all have been about the same, as long as a and b are small. Any combination of a and b with a sum less than 20 would only affect the third decimals of the posterior mean and standard deviation of π.

The same conclusion can also be seen directly from Figure 3. For any given value of π the value of the posterior distribution is obtained from the product of $\pi^5(1 - \pi)^{13}$ from the prior distribution and $\pi^{420}(1 - \pi)^{1410}$ from the data, leaving out the constants for a moment. Since the posterior distribution is almost zero for π less than 0.20 and more than 0.26, the data function $\pi^{420}(1 - \pi)^{1410}$ must be almost zero in the same range. Thus it makes almost no difference what the value is of the prior distribution for those values of π, since the prior distribution is multiplied by almost zero. In the range from 0.20 to 0.26 for π the prior distribution is almost constant, and the posterior distribution is therefore almost entirely determined by the data function in that range. This issue is discussed further in Chapter 5 (on stable estimation).

No prior information. The question arises whether it is possible to have a prior distribution that expresses complete ignorance. Suppose we feel we have absolutely no prior knowledge about what the proportion of Catholics could be. I have argued that using a prior distribution with a=6 and b=14 is the same as having information from a sample of 20 people, with 6 Catholics and 14 non-Catholics as our prior information. If we have no prior information, that would be the same as not having any sample at all representing the prior information. Thus it can be argued that we ought to use a=0 and b=0 for the informationless prior distribution. This gives a prior distribution

$$f(\pi) = C'\pi^{0-1}(1 - \pi)^{0-1}$$

$$= C' \frac{1}{\pi(1 - \pi)} \qquad [17]$$

which is a u-shaped curve.

Another choice for a and b, which is often favored when we have limited prior information about a population proportion, is to let a=1 and b = 1. In that case, $\pi^{a-1}(1-\pi)^{b-1}$ becomes $\pi^{1-1}(1-\pi)^{1-1} = 1$, and the shape of the distribution can be represented by a horizontal line. This is known as the rectangular or uniform distribution, and it essentially implies that every value of π between 0 and 1 is equally likely. Strictly speaking, the probability that a continuous variable takes on a specific value equals zero, and we can only speak of the probability that π lies within intervals. The rectangular distribution tells us that the probability that π falls in an interval of given length is the same no matter where the interval is located in the range from zero to one.

The issue of possible complete ignorance is discussed further in Chapter 6 in the section on informative versus noninformative priors.

Small samples. When we have small samples, the prior distribution becomes more important. This is not surprising since a small sample contains only limited information, and in that case the posterior distribution is not overwhelmingly determined by the data. It is therefore important to have as much prior information as possible when we have limited data.

One way to study the effect of the data and the prior information is to look at the denominator in the expression for the posterior standard deviation of π. The numerator is almost constant for a wide range of values of a and b and the data, unless we are studying values of π close to zero or one. The denominator is the square root of a+b plus the sample size plus one. The contribution of the prior information is a+b, and the contribution of the sample is the sample size. It is therefore not so much a question of how large the sample is as how large n is versus a+b. When a+b is small relative to the sample size, as in the case of the example above, then the effect of a+b is small and exact numerical value is not very important. But when a+b and the sample size are closer to being equal, the importance of the prior distribution begins to equal the importance of the data. This issue is discussed further in Chapter 6 in the section on the effect of the prior distribution.

Comparison with classical methods. A classical statistician would answer the question of how large π is by estimating the parameter, either using a point estimate or a confidence interval. For our example, a point estimate p equals the number of Catholics in the sample divided by the size of the sample, so that p = 420/1830 = 0.2295. A commonly used Bayesian point estimate is the posterior mean. Computed to four decimals it equals 0.2303. Numerically the two are about the same in this example.

A classical 95 percent confidence interval for π is formed by using the normal approximation to the binomial distribution and computing $p \pm 1.96\sqrt{p(1-p)/n}$. This gives the interval from 0.2102 to 0.2488. A 95 percent Bayesian probability interval is already given above; carried to four decimals the interval goes from 0.2111 to 0.2495. Only seldom do we use this much precision, but with four decimals it is possible to show the differences between the intervals. The Bayesian interval lies slightly to the right of the confidence interval, and it is slightly shorter. Both differences are due to the effect of the prior distribution used in the Bayesian analysis.

It is generally the case that with prior distributions based on limited information, the classical confidence intervals and Bayesian probability intervals are numerically close. But their interpretations are conceptually very different. For the confidence interval we can say that if we had many additional samples and constructed a confidence interval from each sample, then about 95 percent of all the intervals would contain the unknown π and the remaining 5 percent would not contain π. Whether or not our one particular interval from 0.21 to 0.25 will contain π, we have no way of knowing. Hopefully it belongs to the larger set of intervals that all contain π. On the other hand, Bayesian analysis permits us to express our initial uncertainties about π in a prior distribution. After the data are known to us we are still uncertain about π, but our uncertainty has been reduced, as expressed in the posterior distribution. We can express our uncertainty about the parameter using probabilities, and the Bayesian probability interval is one way to express this uncertainty. Bayesian analysis permits us to say that the probability equals 0.95 that π lies between 0.21 and 0.25. This is the way many users of confidence intervals want to interpret a confidence interval, but in classical statistical inference such an interpretation is not possible.

Formal theory. As a summary I present the formal theory of Bayesian analysis of a proportion when the prior distribution for the unknown population parameter is specified by the beta distribution with parameters a and b. The prior distribution can be written

$$f(\pi) = \frac{(a+b-1)!}{(a-1)!(b-1)!} \pi^{a-1}(1-\pi)^{b-1} \qquad [18]$$

The prior mean μ' and variance σ'^2 are found from

$$\mu' = \frac{a}{a+b} \qquad \sigma'^2 = \frac{\mu'(1-\mu')}{a+b+1} \qquad [19]$$

If we are able to specify the prior mean μ' and standard deviation σ', the parameters a and b can be computed as

$$a = \mu'\left[\frac{\mu'(1-\mu')}{\sigma'^2} - 1\right] \qquad b = (1-\mu')\left[\frac{\mu'(1-\mu')}{\sigma'^2} - 1\right] \qquad [20]$$

The data are assumed to satisfy the binomial distribution, such that for the true value of π the probability of the data is found from the expression

$$f(x|\pi) = \frac{n!}{x!(n-x)!} \pi^x(1-\pi)^{n-x} \qquad [21]$$

where n is the sample size, x of the observations have the characteristics we are studying and n – x do not.

The prior distribution and the data probability are combined using Bayes' theorem, and it gives the posterior distribution

$$f(\pi|x) = \frac{(n+a+b-1)!}{(x+a-1)!(n-x+b-1)!} \pi^{x+a-1}(1-\pi)^{n-x+b-1} \qquad [22]$$

which is a beta distribution with parameters x + a and n – x + b. The posterior mean μ'' and variance σ''^2 are found from

$$\mu'' = \frac{x+a}{n+a+b} \qquad \sigma''^2 = \frac{\mu''(1-\mu'')}{n+a+b+1} \qquad [23]$$

For reasonably large exponents the beta distribution can be approximated by the normal distribution, and Bayesian probability intervals for π can be found from $\mu \pm z\sigma$, where z is the appropriate value of the standard normal variable. For example, the curve in Figure 1 has $\mu' = 0.30$, $\sigma' = 0.1$ and with $z = 2.00$, we get the interval from 0.10 to 0.50. The function $\pi^5(1 - \pi)^{13}$ equals 0.0000038 for $\pi = 0.5$ and 0.0000025 for $\pi = 0.1$, which means the curve is not entirely symmetric, but the normal approximation is still quite good.

Exact computations of Bayesian probability intervals can be made from the relationship between the beta distribution and the binomial distribution expressed in the equation

$$\text{Prob}(\pi < \pi_0) = \sum_{x=a}^{a+b-1} \begin{bmatrix} a+b-1 \\ x \end{bmatrix} \pi_0^x (1 - \pi_0)^{a+b-1-x} \qquad [24]$$

For the example

$$\text{Prob}(\pi < 0.1) = \sum_{x=6}^{19} \begin{bmatrix} 19 \\ x \end{bmatrix} 0.1^x (1 - 0.1)^{19-x} = 0.009$$

$$\text{Prob}(\pi < 0.5) = \sum_{x=6}^{19} \begin{bmatrix} 19 \\ x \end{bmatrix} 0.5^x (1 - 0.5)^{19-x} = 0.968$$

and thereby $\text{Prob}(0.1 < \pi < 0.5) = 0.968 - 0.009 = 0.959$. The normal approximation gives a probability of 0.954 for the same interval, and the two probabilities are very close.

The beta distribution is not the only possible distribution we can use for the prior distribution in the analysis of a proportion. The beta distribution gives a wide variety of different curves by using different values for a and b, but it is possible to imagine particular prior distributions for π that cannot be expressed as beta distributions. One way to deal with such a case is to divide the range from 0 to 1 into many intervals and use the given prior distribution to find the probability that π is located in each of the intervals. By using, say, the midpoint in each interval as a value for π, we can treat π as a discrete variable and numerically compute the posterior distribution of π by applying Bayes' theorem the same way we did in the first example in Chapter 3, where π was assumed to have only three values.

For further discussion of the analysis of a proportion see Box and Tiao (1973) and Schmitt (1969).

5. BAYESIAN METHODS FOR OTHER PARAMETERS

This chapter contains methods for the Bayesian analysis of means, correlation and regression coefficients, contingency tables, difference between two means, ratio of two variances, and analysis of variance. In each section the analysis is motivated by a simple example, we discuss how we can obtain a prior distribution for the parameter(s) in question and give the posterior distribution for the parameter(s) when the data satisfy certain assumptions.

Mean

As part of their work on social indicators, Campbell and Converse (1980) asked a sample of Americans to rate their standard of living on a thermometer scale from 0 to 100. These data can be used to study the mean value μ of this variable for the entire population.

Bayesian analysis of a population mean requires us to express our uncertainty about the true value of the mean in a prior distribution. The probability of the data for a given value of the mean μ can be found if we know the theoretical distribution for the data in the population from which the data come. Bayes' theorem combines the information from the prior distribution with the information from the data and leaves us with a posterior distribution for μ. The posterior distribution contains all the available information about μ, and it can be used to find point and interval estimates for the unknown μ.

Flat prior distribution. The exact mathematical theory has been worked out for two different prior distributions for μ, the rectangular and the normal, and the example is first discussed using the rectangular distribution. As the name implies, the graph looks like a rectangle, in this case from 0 to 100 with height 1/100, such that the total area under the curve equals one. With this distribution the probability of μ falling in an interval of specific length is the same no matter where the interval is located between 0 and 100, and in everyday terms we interpret that to say that every value of μ is equally likely.

Using the rectangular prior distribution for μ in this example means that we have very little knowledge about how people feel about their standard of living. We are allowing for the possibility that on the average people range from very dissatisfied (0) to very satisfied (100), and the mean could be anywhere between these two extremes.

The data consist of n = 3611 values of the standard of living variable. The histogram for these data is slightly skewed, but it does not violently fail to satisfy the requirement that the data are distributed as a normal distribution. The observed sample mean $\bar{y}$ equals 76.91, and the sample standard deviation s equals 18.46.

The rectangular prior distribution for μ over the range from minus infinity to plus infinity and the prior distribution for σ discussed below combined in Bayes' theorem with data from a normal distribution give a posterior distribution of μ. This posterior distribution is a t distribution with n − 1 degrees of freedom, the mean of μ equals $\bar{y}$, and the standard deviation of μ equals $s/\sqrt{n}$. Using this result in our example, even though μ can range only from 0 to 100, we get

$$t = \frac{\mu - \bar{y}}{s/\sqrt{n}} = \frac{\mu - 76.91}{18.46/\sqrt{3611}} = \frac{\mu - 76.91}{0.31} \qquad [25]$$

The mean of the unknown parameter μ is the known sample mean 76.91, and the standard deviation of μ becomes $18.46/\sqrt{3611} = 0.31$. Since this standard deviation is so small, it makes no difference whether μ ranges from minus to plus infinity or from 0 to 100. For the example, the posterior distribution of μ is the t distribution with 3610 degrees of freedom, and with that many degrees of freedom the t distribution can be replaced by the normal distribution.

From this Bayesian anlysis we can conclude that we are very certain the U.S. population mean for self-reported standard of living scores is close to 76.91. More specifically, the probability equals 0.95 that the U.S. population mean lies between $76.91 - 1.96 \cdot 0.31 = 76.31$ and $76.91 + 1.96 \cdot 0.31 = 77.51$. Other probability intervals can be obtained by replacing z = 1.96 by other percentiles from the normal distribution.

This analysis is done under an additional assumption about the standard deviation of the data variable. Since it is assumed that the variable has a normal distribution, the data distribution is characterized by two parameters. The first parameter is the mean μ, and the prior distribution of μ is assumed to be the rectangular distribution. The second parameter is the standard deviation σ. Since there is a second parameter involved as well, we need a prior distribution for that parameter also.

The result that the posterior distribution for μ is the t distribution is based on the assumption that the prior distribution for the logarithm of the standard deviation is the rectangular distribution and that μ and σ are independent. In most cases this is a very reasonable assumption and not something that needs concern us much. For a further discussion of this point see Jeffreys (1961) and Schmitt (1969).

Finally, if the value of the standard deviation σ for the data variable is known, then we do not need to consider σ as a random variable and no prior distribution is needed for σ. In that case, with a rectangular prior distribution for the mean μ, the posterior distribution is the normal distribution instead of the t distribution, with posterior mean and standard deviation as discussed above.

Normal prior and known σ. Not everyone would use the rectangular distribution as the prior distribution for μ. If someone has more information about how people feel about their standard of living, that information should be incorporated in the prior distribution. Let the prior distribution be a normal distribution instead of the rectangular distribution and the data come from a normal distribution, with a known standard deviation. Then the posterior distribution for the population mean is also a normal distribution. We therefore try to express our prior opinion in a normal distribution, if that is possible, when we are dealing with data from a normal distribution.

As an example, suppose we believe that, on the average, people feel their standard of living is about 50, halfway between the two extremes, and it is as likely that the population mean is less than 50 as more than 50. More specifically, suppose our prior uncertainty about μ can be represented by a normal distribution with mean 50 and standard deviation 15. Thus, two standard deviations equals 30, which leads to the conclusion that we are almost certain the population mean lies somewhere between 20 and 80.

This analysis requires that the variance is known in the population from which the data come. However, when the sample is large, it is possible to use the sample variance s^2 for the population variance σ^2.

With a normal prior distribution for μ and data from a normal distribution, it can be shown that the posterior distribution for μ is also normal. The mean of the posterior distribution is found as a weighted mean of the prior mean μ' and the sample mean $\bar{y}$, where the weights are the inverse of the prior variance σ'^2 and the sample variance σ^2/n. Mathematically this can be expressed in the formula

$$\text{posterior mean} = \mu'' = \frac{\dfrac{1}{\sigma'^2}\,\mu' + \dfrac{1}{\sigma^2/n}\,y}{\dfrac{1}{\sigma'^2} + \dfrac{1}{\sigma^2/n}} \qquad [26]$$

Numerically we get

$$\mu'' = \cfrac{\cfrac{1}{15^2} \cdot 50 + \cfrac{1}{18.46^2/3611} \cdot 76.31}{\cfrac{1}{15^2} + \cfrac{1}{18.46^2/3611}}$$

$$= \frac{0.0044 \cdot 50 + 10.5965 \cdot 76.31}{10.6009} = 76.30$$

Using the inverse of the variances as weights results in a small weight when the variance is large and a large weight when the variance is small. This makes sense, because with a small variance we have little variation and we are much more certain about the corresponding value, while a large variance means we are very uncertain about our mean. In the result above, the posterior mean is almost equal to the sample mean. Thus, almost all the information comes from the data and very little comes from the prior distribution. The weight for the sample mean is very much larger than the weight for the prior mean.

The most important feature of this particular example is that the sample size is so large. The prior distribution affects only the second decimal of the posterior mean, and even the variance σ^2 of the data has very little effect. For $\sigma = 18.46$, which is the observed sample standard deviation, the posterior mean equals 76.30. Trying different values of σ gives almost the same result. For $\sigma = 10$ we get 76.31 for the posterior mean, while $\sigma = 26$ gives 76.29. Thus, the assumption of a known variance for the data is not very important here, when the sample is large, since the posterior mean hardly changes with different values of the standard deviation of the data distribution.

The posterior variance of μ is found by combining the prior variance of μ with the variance of the sample mean, as seen in the formula

$$\sigma''^2 = \cfrac{1}{\cfrac{1}{\sigma'^2} + \cfrac{1}{\sigma^2/n}} \qquad [27]$$

The posterior variance is the inverse of the sum of the inverse variances, which is one-half of the harmonic mean of the two variances. Numerically,

$$\sigma''^2 = \cfrac{1}{\cfrac{1}{15^2} + \cfrac{1}{18.46^2/3611}} = 0.0943$$

Thus the posterior standard deviation for μ equals 0.3071. From equation 25 we know that the standard deviation of the sample mean equals 0.3072, and the prior standard deviation of μ equals 15. If no prior information were available, the posterior standard deviation of μ would equal the standard deviation of the sample mean. The reduction of the standard deviation from 0.3072 to 0.3071 is due to the prior information. This reduction is very small, which is another reflection of the fact that we have very little prior information about the population mean.

For further discussions of Bayesian analysis of population means see, for example, Phillips (1974) and Schmitt (1969).

Classical analysis. Here the sample mean is taken as the random variable and the distribution of the sample mean is the t distribution. The classical statistical analysis takes the known sample mean 76.91 as a point estimate of the unknown population mean μ. The standard error of the sample mean equals $s/\sqrt{n} = 0.31$, and the 95 percent confidence interval for the population mean becomes the interval from $76.91 - 1.96 \cdot 0.31 = 76.31$ to $76.91 + 1.96 \cdot 0.31 = 77.51$. Thus, for a two-sided alternative, the null hypothesis that μ equals any value between 76.31 and 77.51 is not rejected.

It is a general result that the confidence interval for the mean is numerically identical to the Bayesian probability interval obtained with a rectangular prior distribution. With a more informative prior distribution, the Bayesian probability interval is shorter than the confidence interval.

Even if the intervals are numerically identical, the interpretations of the two intervals are conceptually very different. The Bayesian interval, founded on probability as a measure of uncertainty, expresses our uncertainty about the population parameter by stating that the probability equals 0.95 that μ lies between 76.31 and 77.51. The classical confidence interval, on the other hand, is founded on probability as a long-run relative frequency. Therefore, 0.95 of the confidence intervals from many different samples will contain the population mean while the remaining intervals will not. Whether or not the particular interval from 76.31 to 77.51 contains the population mean, we have no way of knowing.

There is considerable reason to believe that many people who construct classical confidence intervals choose secretly to interpret the intervals as Bayesian probability intervals. They reason that since intervals from most samples do contain the unknown population mean, then chances are pretty good our particular interval contains the true parameter value. Thus, they move from using probability as a long-run relative frequency to a personal measure of uncertainty, and they apply a Bayesian interpretation to the interval. But Bayesian and classical inference are conceptually incompatible, and we have to stay within one or the other system, we are not free to move from one to the other in the middle of the analysis. This illustrates, however, the intuitive appeal of Bayesian statistics.

Correlation

The value of a correlation coefficient is by definition restricted to lie somewhere in the interval ranging from -1.00 to $+1.00$. Therefore, the prior and posterior distributions for the correlation coefficient must equal zero outside that interval, and this automatically eliminates the use of distributions like the normal or t distributions, which range from minus to plus infinity. It turns out that the exact distributions for the analysis of correlation coefficients are difficult to work with mathematically for both Bayesian and classical statistics, and transformations and approximations are therefore commonly used.

Let the prior distribution of the population correlation coefficient ρ be the rectangular distribution from -1.00 to $+1.00$, which essentially means that the unknown ρ could be anywhere in that range. The data are assumed to come from a bivariate normal distribution, and the n observed pairs of observations results in a known sample correlation coefficient r. The exact posterior distribution for ρ obtained from Bayes' theorem with a flat prior distribution and normal data is difficult to work with, and instead we use the transformation shown below.

The unknown ρ is changed to a new variable ζ according to the equation

$$\zeta = \frac{1}{2} \ln \frac{1 + \rho}{1 - \rho} \tag{28}$$

where ln stands for the natural logarithm. For middle values of ρ there is very little difference between the two variable ρ and ζ. For example, for ρ between -0.50 and 0.50, the corresponding values of ζ range from

–0.55 to 0.55. But as ρ gets closer to its endpoints, plus and minus one, ζ moves out to plus or minus infinity.

With a rectangular prior distribution and data from the bivariate normal distribution, the posterior distribution for ζ becomes the normal distribution with mean μ'' and variance σ''^2, where

$$\mu'' = \frac{1}{2} \ln \frac{1+r}{1-r} - \frac{5r}{2(n-1)} \qquad \sigma''^2 = \frac{1}{n-1} \qquad [29]$$

This mean and variance can be computed and used to find Bayesian probability intervals for ζ. These intervals can then be transformed back from ζ to ρ and thereby give probability intervals for the unknown ρ, as shown below.

An example. In a random sample of size n = 50 we find a correlation coefficient r = 0.60 for the strength of the relationship between two variables. If the prior distribution of the unknown population correlation coefficient between the two variables is the rectangular distribution from minus one to plus one, what can we conclude about ρ from the posterior distribution?

From the results above we have that the posterior distribution of the transformed variable ζ is the normal distribution with

$$\text{mean} = \frac{1}{2} \ln \frac{1+0.6}{1-0.6} - \frac{5 \cdot 0.6}{2(50-1)} = 0.693 - 0.031 = 0.662$$

and

$$\text{variance} = \frac{1}{50-1} = 0.0204$$

standard deviation = 0.143

A 95 percent Bayesian probability interval for ζ goes from $0.662 - 1.96 \cdot 0.143 = 0.382$ to $0.662 + 1.96 \cdot 0.143 = 0.942$. In order to conclude anything about the population correlation coefficient, we have to get back from ζ to ρ. The endpoints of the interval for ζ have to be transformed back from the ζ scale to the ρ scale. That is done by solving equation 28 for ρ, which gives

$$\rho = \frac{e^{2\zeta} - 1}{e^{2\zeta} + 1} \tag{30}$$

Numerically, when $\zeta = 0.382$ we get

$$\rho = \frac{e^{2 \cdot 0.382} - 1}{e^{2 \cdot 0.382} + 1} = \frac{2.147 - 1}{2.147 + 1} = 0.36$$

Similarly, when $\zeta = 0.942$ we get

$$\rho = \frac{e^{2 \cdot 0.942} - 1}{e^{2 \cdot 0.942} + 1} = \frac{6.580 - 1}{6.580 + 1} = 0.74$$

A point estimate of ρ is the mean of the posterior distribution. The posterior mean of ζ equals 0.622, which translates to $\rho = 0.58$. An interval estimate of ρ consists of the interval from 0.36 to 0.74, and the probability equals 0.95 that ρ lies in that interval.

Note that the interval is quite long. One might have thought that with a sample as large as 50 observations, it would be possible to determine the population correlation coefficient quite precisely, while we have only been able to say that we are almost certain ρ lies somewhere between 0.36 and 0.74.

For a more mathematical discussion of the Bayesian analysis of the correlation coefficient with a rectangular prior distribution see Box and Tiao (1973).

More informative priors. Often we are able to say more about the population correlation than that it lies somewhere between plus and minus one. Earlier research may well have information about ρ that we can use to specify a more informative prior distribution. Using the transformation to the normal distribution shown above then makes it possible to borrow some of the results from the analysis of the mean and arrive at a posterior distribution for ρ. Particularly with small samples does prior information become important.

Continuing the earlier example, suppose our prior knowledge leads us to say that we are almost certain ρ lies between 0.20 and 0.80. By transforming these two values of ρ to the corresponding values of ζ using equation 28, we get

$$\varsigma_L = \frac{1}{2} \ln \frac{1 + 0.20}{1 - 0.20} = 0.203 \qquad \varsigma_U = \frac{1}{2} \ln \frac{1 + 0.80}{1 - 0.80} = 1.099$$

where L and U stand for lower and upper, respectively.

Since ζ is a normally distributed variable, we take ζ_L and ζ_U to be values in the two tails symmetric around the mean, containing almost all the probabilities between them. Therefore, the prior mean of ζ is halfway between the two values, and there are about 4 standard deviations between them. With that, the mean of the prior distribution becomes

$$\mu' = \frac{\varsigma_U + \varsigma_L}{2} = \frac{1.099 + 0.203}{2} = 0.651 \qquad [31]$$

and the prior standard deviation becomes

$$\sigma' = \frac{\varsigma_U - \varsigma_L}{4} = \frac{1.099 - 0.203}{4} = 0.224 \qquad [32]$$

Let the data again consist of a random sample of $n = 50$ observations with a sample correlation coefficient $r = 0.60$. Transformed to the ζ scale let us denote the observed sample value by z, where

$$z = \frac{1}{2} \ln \frac{1 + r}{1 - r} = \frac{1}{2} \ln \frac{1 + 0.60}{1 - 0.60} = 0.693$$

With the observed correlation coefficient transformed to Z, the random variable Z follows a normal distribution with variance

$$\text{var}(z) \approx \frac{1}{n - 3} = \frac{1}{50 - 3} = \frac{1}{47} = 0.0213$$

In the ζ scale we now have a normal prior distribution with mean $\mu' = 0.651$ and variance $\sigma'^2 = 0.224^2 = 0.050$. The data consist of one observation $z = 0.693$ from a normal distribution with variance $\sigma^2 = 0.0213$. The posterior distribution of ζ is therefore normal, and with mean μ'' from equation 26,

$$\mu'' = \frac{\dfrac{1}{0.050}\,0.651 + \dfrac{1}{0.0213}\,0.693}{\dfrac{1}{0.050} + \dfrac{1}{0.0213}}$$

$$= \frac{20 \cdot 0.651 + 47 \cdot 0.0693}{20 + 47} = \frac{45.591}{67} = 0.682$$

and variance σ''^2 from equation 27

$$\sigma''^2 = \frac{1}{\dfrac{1}{0.050} + \dfrac{1}{0.0213}} = \frac{1}{20 + 47} = 0.0149$$

This gives the posterior standard deviation $\sigma'' = 0.122$.

A 95 percent Bayesian probability interval for ζ goes from $\zeta_L = \mu'' - 1.96\sigma''$ to $\zeta_U = \mu'' + 1.96\sigma''$. By substituting, the interval for this example becomes from $\zeta_L = 0.44$ to $\zeta_U = 0.92$.

Finally, transforming this interval back to the ρ scale according to equation 30 gives

$$\rho_L = \frac{e^{2 \cdot 0.44} - 1}{e^{2 \cdot 0.44} + 1} = \frac{1.41}{3.41} = 0.41$$

$$\rho_U = \frac{e^{2 \cdot 0.92} - 1}{e^{2 \cdot 0.92} + 1} = \frac{5.30}{7.30} = 0.73$$

Thus, the probability equals 0.95 that ρ lies between 0.41 and 0.73.

With the rectangular prior distribution for ρ the posterior 95 percent probability interval goes from 0.36 to 0.74, and with our more informative prior distribution the interval goes from 0.41 to 0.73. While this reduction in the length of the interval is not particularly large, it illustrates the effect of a more informative prior distribution. The reason the prior distribution did not have more effect is that it specified only that ρ most likely is in the range from 0.20 to 0.80. This is still a wide range and does not represent much prior knowledge about ρ. But even this limited prior information reduces the length of the 95 percent probability interval by about one-tenth.

Regression

Simple regression. When the relationship between two variables is linear, the slope of the regression line tells us whether the line goes up or down and how steep it is. From our sample data we can compute the slope b for the sample, and we would like to make statements about the slope β of the regression line for the entire population from which the sample was taken in order to understand better the relationship that is being studied.

In Bayesian inference, statements about the unknown β are made using the posterior distribution of β. As for other parameters, this posterior distribution is obtained from Bayes' theorem by combining prior information with information contained in the data.

But β is not the only parameter in the linear regression model, and we need to consider the other two parameters as well. One other parameter is the intercept α of the regression line, and the third is the standard deviation σ of the residuals. All three parameters must be included in the analysis even if we may be interested in only one of them.

Let the prior distribution of β be the rectangular distribution over the range of possible values of β. Similarly, let the prior distribution of α be the rectangular distribution over the range of its possible values. Finally, let the prior distribution of the logarithm of σ be the rectangular distribution over the range of possible values. Taken as variables, since we do not know their true values, assume that β, α, and logarithm of σ are independent of each other. These particular prior distributions are commonly used as the noninformative prior distributions when we have very little information about the three parameters prior to the data collection. With these particular prior distributions and data from a normal distribution, the resulting posterior distributions are particularly simple to work with.

The data are assumed to satisfy the usual assumption of normality. For a fixed value x of the independent variable X the dependent variable is assumed to have a normal distribution with mean $\alpha + \beta x$ and variance σ^2. Thus, for different values of X the means of the dependent variable lie on a straight line. The variance around this line of means is the same σ^2, irrespective of the value of X.

From the data we can compute the observed, sample regression line with intercept a and slope b and the observed variance of the residuals around the regression s^2.

With the rectangular prior distributions from minus to plus infinity and data from normal distributions, it is possible to use Bayes' theorem and find the posterior distributions for the three parameters. In particular, the unknown β has as its posterior distribution the t distribution with mean b, variance $s^2/ \Sigma(x - \bar{x})^2$ and n – 2 degrees of freedom. Thus the known sample slope b is the mean of the probability distribution which specifies our uncertainty about β after the data have been analyzed.

As a point estimate for β we can use the observed sample slope b. A Bayesian probability estimate is obtained from the interval

$$b - t \cdot s/\sqrt{\Sigma(x - \bar{x})^2}$$
$$b + t \cdot s/\sqrt{\Sigma(x - \bar{x})^2}$$

where t is the appropriate percentile from the t distribution with n – 2 degrees of freedom.

Let us continue the example from the section on correlation. There are n = 50 observations, and the observed regression line has the equation

$$y = 10.22 + 1.34x$$

Furthermore, the residual sum of squares equals 3167.43, which means that for the standard deviation of the residuals we get $s = \sqrt{3167.43/48} = 8.12$. We have $\sqrt{\Sigma(x - \bar{x})^2} = 31.50$. The posterior standard deviation of β is therefore equal to $8.12/31.50 = 0.258$. With 48 degrees of freedom t-values of ± 2.01 will give a 95 percent probability interval, which means that the probability is 0.95 that β lies between $1.34 - 2.01 \cdot 0.258 = 0.82$ to $1.34 + 2.01 \cdot 0.258 = 1.86$. For probability values other than 0.95 we would use other t-values.

We are again in the situation that with noninformative prior distributions for the relevant parameters, the Bayesian posterior probability interval for β coincides numerically with the classical confidence interval for that parameter. Thus, if we are presented with a classical confidence interval, as Bayesians we are free to interpret the interval in probabilistic terms the way it is done above.

The posterior distribution of the intercept α is also a t distribution. The mean of α is the known intercept a, the variance of α is $s^2 \Sigma x^2 / n\Sigma(x - \bar{x})^2$, and there are n – 2 degrees of freedom. Numerically we get that the mean of α equals 10.22 and the standard deviation of α equals 1.46. Thus the probability equals 0.95 that α lies between $10.22 - 2.01 \cdot 1.46 = 7.28$ and $10.22 + 2.01 \cdot 1.46 = 13.16$. A 95 percent classical confidence interval would be numerically identical to this interval.

For a more extensive discussion of Bayesian statistical inference in simple regression using noninformative, rectangular prior distributions see Schmitt (1969).

Informative prior for the slope. When the residuals are distributed normally around the regression line with variance σ^2, then the sample slope b has a normal distribution with the variance $Var(b) = \sigma^2 / \Sigma(x - \bar{x})^2$. Thus, we can look at regression analysis as providing us with one data observation with value b of a random variable with variance Var(b).

Let our prior knowledge of the population slope β be expressed as a normal distribution with μ' and variance σ'^2. We are then in the situation that we have a normal prior distribution for the slope, and the data consist of one observation (the observed b) from a normally distributed variable. When we look at regression analysis this way, we can go back to the analysis of a mean and use the results found there. In particular, the posterior distribution of the parameter β becomes a normal distribution with mean

$$\mu'' = \frac{\dfrac{1}{\sigma'^2} \mu' + \dfrac{1}{Var(b)} b}{\dfrac{1}{\sigma'^2} + \dfrac{1}{Var(b)}} \qquad [33]$$

and variance

$$\sigma''^2 = \frac{1}{\dfrac{1}{\sigma'^2} + \dfrac{1}{Var(b)}} \qquad [34]$$

These results are obtained from equations 26 and 27. They are based on the assumption that the variance for the data is known, which here means that the variance of the residuals is known. When this is not the case, we can still use the estimated variance from the data and at least get some sense of the posterior distribution, and the larger the sample is, the better we are able to estimate the population variance.

Continuing the previous example, instead of the rectangular distribution let the prior distribution of the population slope be a normal distribution with mean $\mu' = 2.00$ and standard deviation $\sigma' = 0.75$. Thus, we are almost certain β lies between 0.5 and 3.5. The data consist of the one value b = 1.34, and the estimated standard deviation (standard error) of b equals 0.26. Substituting these values into the equations for the posterior mean and variance, we get that the posterior mean of β equals 1.41 and the posterior standard deviation becomes 0.25. Our uncertainty about β is considerably reduced, since we now are almost certain the value is somewhere between 0.90 and 1.90.

To get a feeling for how sensitive this analysis is to the assumption of a known variance of b, we can try different values for this variance. Above we have the posterior mean and standard deviation of β when the standard deviation of b equals 0.26. If we used 0.30 instead, we find that the posterior mean and standard deviation equal 1.43 and 0.28. For 0.22 the same quantities become 1.39 and 0.21. Thus the posterior mean does not change much, while the posterior standard deviation is more affected.

Multiple regression. A multiple linear regression model with k explanatory variables is characterized by an intercept, a coefficient for each variable and the residual variance, for a total of k + 2 parameters. In theory, a Bayesian analysis calls for a joint, prior distribution of all k + 2 parameters expressing whatever dependencies there might be between the parameters. Such a multivariate prior distribution would be combined with the data distribution in Bayes' theorem, resulting in a multivariate posterior distribution for the parameters. In order to get the posterior distribution for a particular parameter, the joint multivariate posterior distribution has to be manipulated mathematically to eliminate the other parameters.

With rectangular and independent prior distributions for the k + 1 coefficients and the logarithm of the residual standard deviation and data from the multivariate normal distribution, the posterior distribution for each of the regression coefficients is the t distribution with n – k degrees of freedom. The mean of the posterior distribution for the parameter β_i is the observed sample coefficient b_i, and the standard deviation of β_i is the same as the standard deviation for b_i in classical statistical analysis. This is the standard deviation given in the common regression computer packages, but as Bayesians we use it as the standard deviation of β_i instead of for b_i.

For a more detailed and more mathematical discussion of Bayesian inference in multiple regression see Box and Tiao (1973).

Contingency Tables

Contingency tables have not lent themselves easily to Bayesian methods of inference, mainly because of the nonparametric nature of most models for such tables. The classical analysis typically involves the computation of a chi-square statistic under the hypothesis that the sample data come from a population where there is no relationship between the variables. Usually the substantively more important question is how strong the relationship is, and that question is answered by computing one of many possible measures of association, say phi or lambda.

Bayesian inference could focus on one of those measures of association, starting with a prior distribution and combining the prior knowledge with the information in the data to produce a posterior distribution for that parameter. The main difficulty with this plan is the lack of suitable distributions to work with. For example, for a given population value of lambda, it is not clear what the probability is of the data in a particular sample contingency table, and this data probability would be needed for Bayes' theorem.

Because of these difficulties we limit the discussion here to two approaches for the study of 2×2 tables. The first considers the difference between two proportions, and the second deals with the distribution of the phi coefficient.

Difference between two proportions. The analysis of a 2×2 contingency table can often be thought of as the study of the difference between two proportions. Suppose the columns refer to men and women while the rows refer to Democrats and Republicans. The question of whether there is a relationship between the two variables, sex and political party, can be answered by examining whether the proportion of Democrats is different among men and women.

We can start the Bayesian analysis by studying the two proportions separately. Suppose the true population proportion in the first group (men) equals π_1, the prior distribution for π_1 is a beta distribution with parameters a_1 and b_1, the sample consists of n_1 observations, and x_1 of those are of one kind (Democrats) and $n_1 - x_1$ are of the other kind

TABLE 2
Hypothetical Data for Sex and Political Party

		Sex		Total
		Men	Women	
Party	Democrats	$x_1 = 40$	$x_2 = 20$	$r_1 = 60$
	Republicans	10	30	$r_2 = 40$
	Totals	$n_1 = 50$	$n_2 = 50$	$n = 100$
			phi = 0.41	

(Republicans). In the other group (women) the same quantities are denoted π_2, a_2, b_2, n_2, and x_2. Then the posterior distribution for π_1 and π_2 are beta distributions with means μ_1 and μ_2 and variance σ_1^2 and σ_2^2, as shown in equation 23.

From the results given above we have that the posterior mean of $\pi_1 - \pi_2$ equals $\mu_1 - \mu_2$ and the posterior variance of $\pi_1 - \pi_2$ equals $\sigma_1^2 + \sigma_2^2$. With more than just a few observations in each sample, the distribution of $\pi_1 - \pi_2$ can be approximated by a normal distribution, which makes it possible to construct Bayesian probability intervals for the difference between π_1 and π_2.

As a numerical example suppose our prior distributions for π_1 and π_2 are identical and symmetric with $a_1 = a_2 = b_1 = b_2 = 5$. Among the $n_1 = 50$ men there are $x_1 = 40$ Democrats and among the $n_2 = 50$ women there are $x_2 = 20$ Democrats. The posterior distribution for π_1 is then a beta distribution with mean

$$\mu_1'' = \frac{x_1 + a_1}{n_1 + a_1 + b_1} = \frac{40 + 5}{50 + 5 + 5} = \frac{45}{60} = 0.75$$

and variance

$$\sigma_1''^2 = \frac{\mu_1''(1 - \mu_1'')}{n_1 + a_1 + b_1 + 1} = \frac{0.75 \cdot 0.25}{50 + 5 + 5 + 1} = \frac{0.1875}{61} = 0.0031$$

the posterior distribution for π_2 is also a beta distribution, with mean

$$\mu_2'' = \frac{x_2 + a_2}{n_2 + a_2 + b_2} = \frac{20 + 5}{50 + 5 + 5} = \frac{25}{60} = 0.42$$

and variance

$$\sigma_2''^2 = \frac{\mu_2''(1 - \mu_2'')}{n_2 + a_2 + b_2 + 1} = \frac{0.416 \cdot 0.5833}{50 + 5 + 5 + 1} = \frac{0.2431}{61} = 0.0040$$

From these means and variances we find that the difference $\pi_1 - \pi_2$ has posterior mean $0.75 - 0.42 = 0.33$ and posterior variance $0.0031 + 0.0040 = 0.0071$. This gives a posterior standard deviation of 0.084. With samples this large the posterior distribution of $\pi_1 - \pi_2$ can be approximated well by a normal distribution with mean 0.33 and standard deviation 0.084. A 95 percent probability interval for $\pi_1 - \pi_2$ goes from $0.33 - 1.96 \cdot 0.084 = 0.17$ to $0.33 + 1.96 \cdot 0.08 = 0.49$. Thus the probability equals 0.95 that the true difference between the proportion of Democrats among men and women lies somewhere between 0.17 and 0.49.

Distribution of phi. When the expected frequencies in a 2×2 contingency table are large enough for us to compute the classical goodness-of-fit chi square, then the frequency in the upper, left cell of the table has an approximate normal distribution with mean $r_1 n_1 / n$ and variance $r_1 r_2 n_1 n_2 / n^3$, where r_1 and r_2 are the two row totals, n_1 and n_2 the two column totals, and n the table total. Thus, in the example shown in Table 2 the observed value of the normally distributed variable equals 40, and the variance of the variable equals $\sigma^2 = 60 \cdot 40 \cdot 50 \cdot 50 / 100^3 = 6$.

With fixed margins this variance is known, not estimated, and we are in the situation that our data consist of one value of a normally distributed variable with known variance. With a rectangular prior distribution for the mean of this variable, we know that the posterior distribution of the mean is normal with mean equal to the sample mean and variance σ_2^2 / n. Since there is only one observation here, the sample mean equals the one observed value, and the variance equals σ^2.

For the example, the posterior distribution of the quantity which in Table 2 is called x_1 is the normal distribution with mean 40 and variance 6. A 95 percent Bayesian probability interval goes from $40 - 1.96 \cdot \sqrt{6} = 35.20$ to $40 + 1.96 \cdot 6 = 44.80$. The observed value of phi is 0.41. If we replace x_1 by the lower value 35.20 and keep the same margins, the resulting value of phi becomes 0.21. If we use the upper value 44.8, phi becomes 0.60. Thus, we are 95 percent certain that phi for the relationship between these two variables lies between 0.21 and 0.60.

Finally, if we had reason to believe that the prior distribution of x_1 was normal with given mean and variance, that information could be combined with the data information. The result would be a posterior normal distribution where the mean would be a weighted mean of the prior mean and the observed data x_1, and the variance would be the inverse of the sum of the inverse variances, as seen in equations 26 and 27.

Difference Between Two Means

Are there differences in incomes between men and women? Do Protestants and Catholics score differently on attitudes toward abortion? These and many similar questions involve the study of the difference between two means from two independent groups of observations. The two groups are defined by a dichotomous nominal variable, and we are asking if there is a relationship between the nominal variable and an interval dependent variable.

One way to examine the relationship between a nominal variable with two categories and an interval variable is to create a dummy variable for the nominal variable and do a regression analysis of the dependent variable on the dummy variable. If the dummy variable has two values 0 and 1, the slope of the regression line will equal the difference between the means of the dependent variable for the two groups, and we can use the method discussed above in the section on regression analysis in order to study the difference between the two means.

Historically, the more common approach to the study of the difference between two means is to develop the method from first principles. However, the resulting formulas are completely equivalent to those used in regression analysis under the usual assumptions of normally distributed variables. As in classical statistical inference, we distinguish between three cases depending upon the variances in the two populations from which the data come: when the two variances are known, when the two variances are unknown and equal, and when the two variances are unknown and unequal.

Known variances. In the unusual case when the two groups of observations are samples from populations where the two variances σ_1^2 and σ_2^2 are known, we can work directly with the difference between the two population means $\delta = \mu_1 - \mu_2$. The observed difference d between the two sample means has a normal distribution with variance

$$\text{Var(d)} = \text{Var}(\bar{y}_1 - \bar{y}_2) = \frac{\sigma_1^2}{n_1} + \frac{\sigma_2^2}{n_2} \qquad [35]$$

where n_1 and n_2 are the two sample sizes.

We can now use the various results from the section on the analysis of a single mean. With a rectangular prior distribution for δ, the resulting posterior distribution is a normal distribution with mean d and variance $\sigma_1^2/n_1 + \sigma_2^2/n_2$ from equation 35. With a normal prior distribution for δ with mean μ' and variance σ'^2, the mean of the normal posterior distribution is the weighted mean of μ' and d where the weights are the inverses of the corresponding variances, as shown in equation 26. Similarly, the posterior variance is the inverse of the sum of the inverse variances, as shown in equation 27.

Unknown, equal variances. Is there a difference in appearance between middle-class and working-class girls? This question was examined in the Oakland Growth Study and the results are reported in Elder (1969). Thirty-five middle-class girls and 43 working-class girls were measured on a variable called good physique, and the middle-class girls had a mean score of 56.6 and a standard deviation of 13.5, while the corresponding results for the working-class girls were 48.6 and 14.2.

We assume that the variances σ_1^2 and σ_2^2 in the two populations are equal, so that $\sigma_1^2 = \sigma_2^2 = \sigma^2$ and that μ_1, μ_2, and log σ are independent. Let the prior distributions for the two population means μ_1 and μ_2 and log σ be rectangular. With data from normal distributions it can be shown that the posterior distribution for $\delta = \mu_1 - \mu_2$ is the t distribution with mean d = $\bar{y}_1 - \bar{y}_2$, and variance $s^2(1/n_1 + 1/n_2)$, where s^2 is the pooled variance from the two samples, and $n_1 + n_2 - 2$ degrees of freedom.

For our example, the pooled variance becomes

$$s^2 = \frac{(35-1)13.5^2 + (43-1)14.2^2}{35 + 43 - 2} = \frac{14665.38}{76} = 192.9655$$

The posterior variance of δ becomes 192.9655(1/35 + 1/43) = 10.0009, which means that the posterior standard deviation becomes 3.16. The posterior mean of δ equals 56.6 – 48.6 = 8.0, and the t distribution has 76 degrees of freedom. Thus, the probability equals 0.95 that δ lies between

$8.0 - 1.99 \cdot 3.16 = 1.71$ and $8.0 + 1.99 \cdot 3.16 = 14.29$. Furthermore, if δ is larger than zero, the population mean for middle-class girls is larger than the population mean for working-class girls. This would mean that, on the average, middle-class girls are thought to have a better appearance than working-class girls. The t value for $\delta = 0$ becomes

$$t = \frac{0 - 0.80}{3.16} = -2.53$$

and the probability that t is larger than -2.53 equals 0.99. Thus, the probability equals 0.99 that the mean for middle-class girls is larger than the mean for working-class girls in Oakland, as measured by the staff of that study.

The Bayesian probability interval from 1.71 to 14.29 is numerically identical to the 95 percent confidence interval obtained from classical statistics, even though the interpretations of the two intervals are conceptually very different. What this means, however, is that as Bayesians we are free to interpret a classical confidence interval for the difference between two means as the Bayesian probability interval we get from rectangular prior distributions and the observed data.

Unknown, unequal variances. When the two sets of observations come from populations where the variances σ_1^2 and σ_2^2 are unequal, the t distribution no longer applies.

Let μ_1, μ_2, $\log \sigma_1$, and $\log \sigma_2$ be independent with rectangular prior distributions. The data in the first sample are drawn from a normal distribution with mean μ_1 and variance σ_1^2, and the data in the second sample are drawn from a normal distribution with parameters μ_2 and σ_2^2. Looking at the two parameters μ_1 and μ_2 separately, we know from the section above on a single mean that the posterior distributions for both means are t distributions.

But we want the posterior distribution for the difference between μ_1 and μ_2, and that distribution is not a t distribution because of the unequal variances. It is possible to show that the posterior distribution we want is the Behrens-Fisher distribution. But it is not a distribution that is easy to work with, and we can approximate the Behrens-Fisher distribution by a t distribution. This approximation involves modifying the posterior variance of $\mu_1 - \mu_2$ and the degrees of freedom.

The approximation requires us to find two numbers a and b. The posterior distribution of $\mu_1 - \mu_2$ is then approximately a t distribution with mean $\bar{y}_1 - \bar{y}_2$, variance $a^2(s_1^2/n + S_2^2/n)$ and b degrees of freedom. As an example, let us use the same data on the Oakland girls. Following Box and Tiao (1973), the computations proceed as follows in order to find a and b:

$$u = \frac{s_1^2/n_1}{s_1^2/n_1 + s_2^2/n_2} = \frac{13.5^2/35}{13.5^2/35 + 14.2^2/43} = \frac{5.207}{9.896} = 0.526$$

$$v = 1 - u = 1 - 0.526 = 0.474$$

$$f_1 = \frac{n_1 - 1}{n_1 - 3} u + \frac{n_2 - 1}{n_2 - 3} v = \frac{34}{32} 0.526 + \frac{42}{40} 0.474 = 1.057$$

$$f_2 = \frac{(n_1 - 1)^2}{(n_1 - 3)^2 (n_1 - 5)} u^2 + \frac{(n_2 - 1)^2}{(n_2 - 3)^2 (n_2 - 5)} v^2$$

$$= \frac{34^2}{32^2 \cdot 30} 0.526^2 + \frac{42^2}{40^2 \cdot 38} 0.474^2 = 0.017$$

$$b = 4 + \frac{f_1^2}{f_2} = 4 + \frac{1.057^2}{0.017} = 71.6$$

$$a = \frac{b - 2}{b} f_1 = \frac{71.6 - 2}{71.6} 1.057 = 1.027 \qquad [36]$$

Thus, the posterior distribution of $\mu_1 - \mu_2$ is approximated by a t distribution with mean $\bar{y}_1 - \bar{y}_2 = 56.6 - 48.6 = 8.0$, variance $a^2(s_1^2/n_1 + s_2/n_2) = 1.027^2(13.5^2/35 + 14.2^2/43) = 10.44$, and $b \approx 72$ degrees of freedom. These results are not very different from the results obtained under the assumption of equal variances, which is not surprising since the two observed sample variances $s_1^2 = 13.5^2 = 182.25$ and $s_2 = 14.2^2 = 201.64$ are almost equal. But the computations illustrate what magnitudes of adjustments we get even with small differences between the two observed sample variances.

There is no similar result available from classical statistics.

Ratio of Two Variances

Sometimes there are substantive reasons for comparing two variances—for example, if we want to find out if one group is more homogeneous than another with respect to some variable. But, more often, we are interested in the difference between two means, and we need to compare the variances first to determine which method to use for the comparison of the means.

We have data from two normal distributions with means μ_1 and μ_2 and variances σ_1^2 and σ_2^2. Let μ_1, μ_2, $\log \sigma_1$, and $\log \sigma_2$ be independent and with rectangular prior distributions. It then follows from Bayes' theorem that the posterior distribution of the ratio

$$F = \frac{s_1^2/s_2^2}{\sigma_1^2/\sigma_2^2} \qquad [37]$$

is the F distribution with $n_1 - 1$ and $n_2 - 1$ degrees of freedom, where s_1^2 and s_2^2 are the observed sample variances and n_1 and n_2 the two sample sizes.

Continuing our example from the previous section we have that

$$F = \frac{13.5^2/14.2^2}{\sigma_1^2/\sigma_2^2} = \frac{0.90}{\sigma_1^2/\sigma_2^2}$$

has the F distribution with 34 and 42 degrees of freedom. This result does not directly provide us with the posterior distribution of σ_1^2/σ_2^2, even though it is possible to obtain that distribution, as shown in Box and Tiao (1973).

Another approach consists of using the F distribution to get Bayesian probability intervals for σ_1^2/σ_2^2. From the table of the F distribution it is possible to find two values F_L and F_U such that the probability equals $1 - \alpha$ that the random variable F lies between F_L and F_U. In other words, the probability equals $1 - \alpha$ that

$$F_L < F < F_U$$

where F_L is in the left tail and F_U is in the right tail of the F distribution. Substituting for F we get

$$F_L < \frac{s_1^2/s_2^2}{\sigma_1^2/\sigma_2^2} < F_U$$

Solving these two inequalities for σ_1^2/σ_2^2 gives us

$$\frac{s_1^2/s_2^2}{F_U} < \sigma_1^2/\sigma_2^2 < \frac{s_1^2/s_2^2}{F_L}$$

For our example,

$$\frac{0.90}{F_U} < \sigma_1^2/\sigma_2^2 < \frac{0.90}{F_L}$$

All we need to do is to find F_L and F_U.

If we want a 95 percent probability interval, then $\alpha = 0.05$. One way to choose F_L and F_U is such that the probability equals 0.975 that F is less than F_U and equals 0.025 that F is less than F_L. This gives a probability of 0.95 that F lies between F_L and F_U. The larger value, F_U, can be found directly from the 97.5 percent F table. With 34 and 42 degrees of freedom we find $F_U = 1.89$. But the left tail of the F distribution is usually not tabulated, and an extra step is therefore needed in order to find F_L. We reverse the degrees of freedom such that we have $n_2 - 1 = 42$ and $n_1 - 1 = 34$ degrees of freedom and look up the corresponding F value in the 97.5 percent table. F_L then equals the inverse of that value. For 42 and 34 degrees of freedom we find $F = 1.94$, which gives us $F_L = 1/1.94 = 0.52$.

The 95 percent Bayesian probability interval for σ_1^2/σ_2^2 becomes

$$0.90/1.89 < \sigma_1^2/\sigma_2^2 < 0.52$$

$$0.48 < \sigma_1^2/\sigma_2^2 < 1.73$$

Thus, we are 95 percent certain that the ratio between the two population variances lies between 0.48 and 1.73.

One minor point. F_L and F_U were found by excluding 2.5 percent in the left tail and 2.5 percent in the right tail of the F distribution to give us a 95 percent probability interval. But the F distribution is skewed, and because of that the interval from F_L to F_U is not the shortest 95 percent probability interval we could have. For example, if we excluded 2 percent in the left tail and 3 percent in the right tail we would still have a 95 percent interval, but that interval would be a little bit shorter, However, for most practical applications the various intervals are not very different, and this is not an issue that need concern us much.

Analysis of Variance

The term "analysis of variance" covers a variety of statistical models for the analysis of the relationship between one or more nominal variables and an interval variable. Depending on how many nominal variables there are, we have a one-way, two-way, or more analysis. In classical statistics we also distinguish between random and fixed effects models. In Bayesian statistics all unknown parameters are considered as random variables, which means that the same distinction between random and fixed effects models does not hold. However, by suitable choices of prior distributions for the relevant parameters, it is possible to derive methods that correspond to the classical distinction between the two types of models. We restrict ourselves here to a one-way analysis of the comparison of the means from several groups, extending the section on the comparison of two means. For a further discussion of a variety of analysis of variance models see Box and Tiao (1973).

In their paper on analysis of variance, Iversen and Norpoth (1976) have a small hypothetical example with n = 18 observations on a variable measuring subjective political competence for samples of respondents from k = 5 different countries. The five country means are 4, 6, 2, 7, and 5, and the observed F ratio equals 13.00 on 4 and 13 degrees of freedom. The conclusion, according to classical statistics, is that with a 1 percent significance level the critical F value equals 5.20, and since the observed value of F is larger than 5.20, the null hypothesis of equal population means is rejected.

Let us now look at a Bayesian analysis of the same question of whether the five population means are equal, using the same data. As prior distributions for the five population means and the logarithm of standard deviation of the residuals we use independent rectangular distributions. The data are assumed to be sampled from normal

58

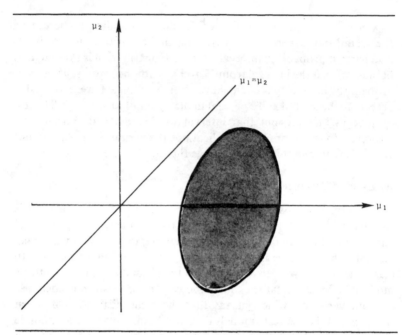

Figure 4: Joint Bayesian Probability Set (Shaded Area) for Two Means and μ_1 and μ_2 with the Subset (Line) for Which $\mu_1 = \mu_2$.

distributions with unknown means and a common variance. Bayes' theorem can then be used to find the joint posterior distribution for the population means. In order to study whether the five population means are equal, we construct from the posterior distribution a joint Bayesian probability set containing the most likely set of values of the five population means, just as we have constructed Bayesian probability intervals for single parameters.

It is difficult to illustrate a joint Bayesian probability set for five population means since it is located in five dimensions. But it is possible to illustrate such a probability set if we were dealing with only two population means μ_1 and μ_2. The shaded area in Figure 4 shows, say, the 99 percent probability set obtained from the joint posterior distribution of μ_1 and μ_2. This means that the point with coordinates (μ_1, μ_2) has a probability of 0.01 of being outside the shaded area.

In analysis of variance we are often particularly interested in whether the population means are equal, here whether $\mu_1 = \mu_2$. Such a restriction on the parameters that they should be equal defines a subset in the μ_1, μ_2 plane. Here this subset is the line through the origin with slope equal to one, marked $\mu_1 = \mu_2$ in Figure 4. For any point on this line the two population means are equal. The figure is drawn in such a way that the line does not intersect the probability set. Therefore, the probability equals 0.99 that the two population means are unequal.

Going back to five dimensions again, the question becomes whether the joint posterior Bayesian probability set for the five population means $\mu_1, \mu_2, \mu_3, \mu_4,$ and μ_5 intersects the subset defined by all the means being equal; that is, the subset defined by $\mu_1 = \mu_2 = \mu_3 = \mu_4 = \mu_5$. This may seem like a difficult question to answer, but it can be shown that the answer depends entirely upon the observed value of the F ratio.

Roughly speaking, the subset of equal population means intersects the Bayesian probability set of likely parameter values only if the observed F is small. Similarly, if the observed F is large, then the subset of equal means does not intersect the probability set. Thus, a small value of F allows for the possibility that the population means are equal, while a large F is evidence that not all the means are equal.

More specifically, the subset of equal population means intersects the P percent probability set if and only if the observed value of F is less than the Pth percentile of the F distribution. For our example, using P equal to 99, the subset of equal population means intersects the 99 percent probability set if and only if the observed value of F is less than 5.20, which is the ninety-ninth percentile of the F distribution with 4 and 13 degrees of freedom. The data gave F = 13.00, and the situation is like the one illustrated in Figure 4. The "line" defined by the equality of the five means does not intersect the 99 percent probability set; the probability therefore equals 0.99 that the five population means are not equal.

6. PRIOR DISTRIBUTIONS

Prior distributions are used in all the Bayesian methods and examples above, and in this chapter we take a closer and more systematic look at various aspects of these distributions.

The first exposure to prior distributions occurs in the presentation of Bayes' theorem in Chapter 3, where the theorem is used to distinguish between three different populations. There are times when several different populations actually exist, and the choice of which one to draw the data from is determined by some probabilistic mechanism like the toss of a die. Each of the three populations in the example has equal prior probabilities of one-third. In such a case, even a classical statistician would use Bayes' theorem to determine the probabilities, after the data are known, of the various populations' being the source of the data. But when we are dealing with only a single population whose parameters have unknown values, then only Bayesian inference makes use of prior distributions. In such cases classical inference has no similar concept.

In that first example the prior probabilities are informative, and they reflect some very specific knowledge about the populations. Particularly if the probabilities are unequal and one population has a much higher probability than the other, then we know a good deal about which population might have generated the data even before the data are collected. This is in contrast with some of the later examples, where we often use rectangular prior distributions to reflect the fact that we have very limited prior knowledge.

A second feature of the example with three different populations is that the prior probabilities are easy to find. They are determined directly from the probabilities of the various outcomes of the toss of a well-balanced die. More often, prior probabilities are harder to determine. For example, sometimes prior probabilities are found by first determining specific values of the parameter in the prior distribution. The beta distribution is one of those distributions, and for that distribution we must specify numerical values of the two parameters a and b.

A third feature of the same example is that there is nothing subjective about the choice of the prior probabilities. When they are determined by a probability mechanism like the toss of a die, all of us would come up with the same values for the prior probabilities. Since there are no ambiguities about such prior probabilities, they can perhaps be thought of as being more "scientific" than when each of us has different prior probability distributions. After all, the results from a scientific research project should not depend upon who did the research. However, as discussed below, Bayesians do not see it as a problem that people may have different prior distributions.

The final question to be discussed about prior distributions is how much effect they have on the posterior distributions. In the example referred to above with three different populations with equal prior probabilities, in some sense the prior probabilities had very little effect. This is because, in the computations shown in Table 1, they cancel out in the numerator and denominator of Bayes' theorem, and the posterior probabilities are directly proportional to the data probabilities. But the sample is very small in that example, and other prior distributions would have produced very different posterior distributions.

Informative versus Noninformative Priors

Two conflicting arguments are discussed in this section. One argument is that we are doing research on a problem because we do not know the answers to the problem, and through our research we explore new grounds and unknown territories. The aim of the research is to establish the value of some unknown parameter—say, the slope of a regression line—in order to understand how two variables are related. The research is done in order to replace our ignorance about the parameter with information about what the value of the parameter might be.

Bayesian analysis requires a prior distribution for the unknown parameter. Even if we are truly ignorant about the parameter, we do need a prior distribution. This raises the two questions of whether there is something called complete ignorance and, if so, can such ignorance be expressed in a prior distribution. Personally I am completely ignorant about many things, and I expect I am not alone in that situation.

But expressing complete ignorance in a prior distribution is another matter. A person may well say, "I have no idea what the value is of that regression coefficient. As far as I know, any value of the coefficient is possible and no value is more probable than any other value." Hidden in that statement is the notion of a rectangular distribution over the possible range of values for the unknown parameter. But even the rectangular distribution and the quoted sentences represent some information about the parameter. Saying that each value is equally likely is to say something about the parameter and represents a step up from complete ignorance.

The rectangular distribution itself also implies more than complete ignorance. One way to see that is through the following contradiction. Suppose we have a rectangular distribution for a variable X over the range from 0 to 5. The probability of a value of X less than 2.5 is then equal to 0.50. But if I am completely ignorant about X, then I am equally ignorant about X^2. If ignorance is represented by the rectangular distribution, then a rectangular distribution over the range from 0 to 25 should be used for our ignorance about X^2. The probability that X^2 is less than 12.5 is therefore equal to 0.50. From this it follows that the probability also equals 0.50 that X itself is less than $\sqrt{12.5} = 3.54$. But, according to the original rectangular distribution for X, the probability equals 0.50 that X is less than 2.5. The probability cannot equal 0.50 that X is less than 2.5 as well as less than 3.54. These two probability statements about X, based on rectangular distributions for X and X^2, contradict each other and show that the rectangular distribution cannot be used to represent complete ignorance.

Instead of trying to deal with any notion of complete ignorance, we distinguish between informative and noninformative prior distributions. A noninformative prior distribution can be thought of as the lowest level of prior opinion about the parameter being studied, and most often the rectangular distribution is used as such a prior distribution. Instead of trying to express complete ignorance, we express the idea that all values of the parameters are thought to be equally likely over the relevant range of values of the parameter. More specifically, we say an interval of values of fixed length is equally likely no matter where the interval is located within the relevant range of the parameter.

As we see in many of the examples of the use of Bayesian statistics in Chapters 4 and 5, noninformative prior distributions lead to results that numerically correspond to those obtained from classical statistics. Specifically, Bayesian probability intervals correspond numerically to classical confidence intervals. The interpretations of the two types of intervals are widely different, but their correspondence shows that a simple step from the results from classical inference to the results from Bayesian statistical inference can be taken by making use of rectangular prior distributions.

The argument against the rectangular prior distribution and noninformative prior distributions in general is that there is always some available prior probabilistic knowledge, which should be expressed in an informative prior distribution. It can be claimed that research is never done in a vacuum, and if nothing were known about a parameter we would not have thought of doing the research in the first place.

Research is cumulative, and one of the main strengths of Bayesian over classical inference is that it permits the use of knowledge from earlier research in the analysis of results from new research. This implies that we should seek out prior knowledge and express such knowledge in informative prior distributions as part of our research. How we may find such distribuitons and the effects they have is discussed below.

A special case of informative prior distributions exists when we are replicating or building on an old study where the analysis was done using Bayesian inference. In such a case we would simply take the posterior distribution from the previous study and use it as the prior distribution in the new study. A small example of this process is shown in the presentation of Bayes' theorem in Chapter 3, where we first have a sample of one observation, and after that we collected a new sample of ten additional observations. The posterior distribution from the first analysis was used as the prior distribution in the second analysis, and the final posterior distribution is identical to the one we would have obtained after a single analysis of all eleven observations.

The most informative prior distribution we can have is one that assigns a probability of zero to some of the parameter values, because this means it is impossible for the parameter to take on those values. For example, the beta distribution is by definition set equal to zero for values less than zero or larger than one, because the parameter π can only take on values between those two extreme values. The difficulty arises if we assign a zero probability to some subset of possible parameter values. For example, we may allow a regression coefficient to have positive values only and assign zero probability to all negative values. This can create difficulties because, if we are so certain that the parameter cannot be negative, then it does not matter how strong the empirical evidence is in favor of a negative coefficient. The posterior probability will always equal zero for parameter values that have zero prior probability, no matter what information we get from the data. In other words, we feel so strongly that no matter how strong the empirical evidence, we will not change our mind.

The reason the posterior probability is zero for any value of the parameter that has a zero prior probability lies in the nature of Bayes' theorem. The numerator of the theorem consists of the product of the data probability, using that particular parameter value, and the corresponding prior probability for that value of the parameter. If the particular prior probability equals zero, then the entire product in the numerator becomes zero and the fraction itself equals zero, meaning a zero posterior probability.

This means we have to guard against inadvertently assigning zero prior probabilities to parameter values that could possibly be relevant. But as long as the prior probabilities are nonzero, however small, we are assured that the information from the data will properly count toward the determination of the posterior probabilities.

The question of whether we should use a noninformative or an informative prior distribution is important only as long as the choice makes a difference for the posterior distribution. As we see in the section on the effect of the prior distribution at the end of this chapter, the more data we have, the less important is the prior distribution unless we have assigned extremely small prior probabilities to subsets of parameter values.

Finding Prior Distributions

In the first example in Chapter 3 there are three actual populations, and we decided to let each population have a probability of one third of being chosen as the source for the data. Following the Bayesian analysis of the first observation, we collected an additional sample of ten observations. In that case the posterior distribution from the first analysis is used as the prior distribution for the second analysis. In the second case the prior distribution is found without any difficulties.

Specifying prior distributions is seldom that simple, and here we take a closer look at how we may find prior distributions. One important consideration is that our prior distribution should accurately display our prior information about the parameter. At the same time, it should also be as easy as possible to work with. These two requirements may be in conflict. This is not so much an issue when the parameter is discrete and can take on only a few values. In that case the computations of the posterior distribution can be done as outlined in the computations shown in Table 1. Such computations can easily be programmed on a computer.

The difficulty arises when the parameter is treated as a continuous variable, as is the case for a population proportion or a mean. For parameters like that, the prior distribution can be drawn as a continuous curve, and Bayes' theorem can use the mathematical function for that curve in order to produce the posterior distribution. Mathematically, certain functions are easier to work with than others, and we naturally prefer those functions if we can use them. These particular prior distributions are known as *conjugate* prior distributions, and we have several examples of such conjugate distributions in Chapters 4 and 5, even though they were not called by that name.

To illustrate the idea of a conjugate prior distribution, let us look briefly again at the Bayesian analysis of a population proportion π. For a given value of the parameter and binomial data with n observations and x successes, the probability of the data is expressed in the binomial distribution

$$f(x|\pi) = \binom{n}{x} \pi^x (1 - \pi)^{n-x} \qquad [38]$$

Since the data are known, π is the only unknown in this expression. An example of such an equation is shown in equation 14. The numerator in Bayes' theorem consists of the product of this expression and the prior distribution $f(\pi)$.

The question becomes what mathematical function to use such that the product of the data probability in equation 38 and the prior distribution would be particularly simple to find. Mathematics provides us with many, many possible functions, such as polynomial, trignometric, and exponential functions. But a little thought tells us that the one to use here is of the form

$$f(\pi) = C'\pi^{a-1}(1 - \pi)^{b-1} \qquad a > 0, \; b > 0 \qquad [39]$$
$$0 < \pi < 1$$

where C' is a constant computed from the two numbers a and b. An example of such a function is shown in equation 9. The -1's in the two exponents are there for practical reasons and need not concern us here.

The product $f(x|\pi)f(\pi)$ of the expressions in equations 38 and 39 is particularly simple to find since all we need to do is to multiply the binomial coefficient and C', add the exponents for π and add the exponents for $1 - \pi$. Because of that, the posterior distribution involves the terms π and $1 - \pi$ with the appropriate exponents. The posterior distribution for the same example referred to above is seen in equation 16. Thus, both the prior and posterior distributions for π are beta distributions.

We have shown that when we start with a beta distribution as the prior distribution for the population proportion π and when the data satisfy the assumptions for the binomial distribution, then the posterior distribution for π is also a beta distribution. The beta distribution is therefore known as the conjugate prior distribution for π when the data are binomial. Another example of a conjugate prior distribution occurs in the analysis of the mean from a normal distribution. In Chapter 5 we find that if the prior distribution for the mean is a normal distribution, and the data come from a normal distribution with known variance, then the posterior distribution of the mean is also a normal distribution. Thus the normal distribution is known as the conjugate prior distribution for the population mean when the data are normal.

When conjugate prior distributions exist, we try to use them because of the way they simplify finding the posterior distributions. Very little computation is needed, and from Bayes' theorem we know the form of the posterior distribution directly.

But even the presence of a conjugate prior distribution does not answer the question of the exact specification of the prior distribution. In the case of a beta distribution we need to specify the two numbers a and b, and in the case of a normal prior distribution we need the mean and variance of that distribution. These constants determine the exact distribution, and they have to come from the subject matter expert.

It may seem difficult to produce two numbers a and b from some limited, diffuse knowledge about a population proportion, but even a small amount of interrogation may produce a prior distribution. If the expert is willing to say "Based on what I know, I am almost certain the proportion lies between 0.3 and 0.7," we could translate that to say that the prior mean equals 0.5 and the prior standard deviation equals 0.1. This is because plus and minus two standard deviations from the mean will take us to 0.3 and 0.7, and usually plus and minus two standard deviations take in almost all the probability. According to equation 13 this results in a and b both equal to 12, and we have our prior distribution. For an entertaining and more detailed discussion of the kinds of interrogation that can be used to find prior distributions see Raiffa (1968).

Subjective Nature of Priors

A prior distribution expresses the analyst's opinion of a population parameter before any new data are available. Information about parameters is typically limited and can vary from one person to the next. Prior distributions are therefore subjective, meaning that different people analyzing the same problem could well have different prior distributions.

Different prior distributions in themselves would not create any difficulties. But when different prior distributions are applied to the same data, they will produce different posterior distributions, and that can be seen as a problem. How can we permit a method of statistical inference that leads people to different conclusions from the same data?

Bayesian inference is not alone in having subjective choices affect the analysis. In classical testing of a null hypothesis the conclusion is either that the hypothesis is rejected or it is not rejected. Faced with the same data and the same value of the appropriate test statistic, it may well be that one analyst concludes the null hypothesis should be rejected while another analyst concludes it should not be rejected. The decision to reject or not is completely dependent upon how large the rejection region is for the test statistic, and the rejection region is determined by the size of the significance level.

To the extent that the significance level determines whether the hypothesis is rejected or not and the level is subjectively chosen, it becomes subjective whether a null hypothesis is rejected or not. It may be argued that since all social scientists use a 5 percent significance level anyway, everyone would make the same decision about the null hypothesis. But this argument does not deny the fact that rejection or not is completely dependent upon the choice of significance level, and a null hypothesis that is rejected by one analyst is not necessarily rejected by another.

Bayesian inference is subjective in a different way. It reflects the very human fact that if two people have different opinions about something, then even the same limited empirical facts will modify these opinions differently. It is like a Democrat and Republican being faced with the same unemployment figure: The Democrat says the figure shows we need more government intervention and new public programs, while the Republican says the private sector is doing well and will be able to solve the problem. Honest disagreements like this are found all the time, even though the empirical facts are the same for both sides of the arguments. The facts are seen differently because people bring prior convictions to bear on the facts.

Because of differences in training and experiences, one would expect that social scientists also bring different prior distributions to the same problem. Particularly if the prior distributions are very informative and the new information in the data is limited, the posterior distributions will necessarily differ. But the prior distributions bring the subjective aspects of the analysis out in the open for everyone to see. The analyst is forced to express personal opinion and biases in the prior distribution for the world to see, which actually makes the whole analysis less subjective.

There is no right or wrong prior distribution; all we try to do is express our limited prior knowledge in terms of probabilities. The analyst's prior distribution is the expression of one person's opinion, and there is no reason why each reader or listener to the research report could not use his or her own prior distribution. This would give individual posterior distributions, all brought closer to each other than was the case with the prior distributions because of the common data.

To reduce the subjective aspect of prior distributions, it is possible to use a noninformative prior distribution like the rectangular distribution. This still represents a choice of a particular distribution, but it is a more neutral one representing a minimum of prior opinion. While such a distribution may well be a good choice in many situations, there is also no reason we should shy away from our personal choice of a more informative distribution if we have information that warrants such a choice. This is especially the case if the prior distribution plays an important role in the determination of the posterior distribution.

Effect of Priors

The final and perhaps most important question is, How important are the prior distributions? They are conceptually indispensable and provide the foundation on which Bayesian analysis rests, but they are not always important in determining the exact shape of the posterior distributions.

One way to examine the effects of prior distributions is to consider some of the formulas from earlier chapters. For example, from equation 23 we have that the posterior mean of the beta distribution for the study of a population proportion can be expressed $(a + x)/(a + b + n)$. The two quantities a and b come from the prior distribution, and x and n are obtained from the data. If a and b are small relative to x and n, the value of the fraction will not change much for different a's and b's. In that case the prior distribution has very little effect.

Another way to see the same thing is to rewrite the posterior mean as is shown on the right side of the equation

$$\frac{a+x}{a+b+n} = \frac{\frac{a}{a+b}(a+b) + \frac{x}{n}(n)}{a+b+n}$$

$$= \frac{\text{prior estimate} \cdot \text{prior weight} + \text{data estimate} \cdot \text{data weight}}{\text{sum of the weights}} \quad [40]$$

The estimate from the prior distribution of the population proportion is the fraction $a/(a + b)$, and the estimate from the data alone is x/n. On the right side of equation 40 we have a weighted mean of these two estimates. The weight for the prior estimate is $a + b$, and the weight for the estimate from the data is n. Both $a/(a + b)$ and x/n are fractions and therefore numbers between zero and one, and what matters in equation 40 is the size of $a + b$ relative to n. Even a fairly informative prior distribution would not have $a + b$ larger than—say, 20 or 30—and if the sample size is about the same, then the prior distribution is important. But if we are dealing with a large sample—say, a national survey of 1500 respondents—then the expression will be dominated by the data, and the prior distribution with small a and b has absolutely no effect on the substantive result.

The same result is obtained if we consider the posterior variance in equation 23. For a wide range of values of the posterior mean the numerator for the variance is essentially constant, and what matters for the variance is the size of the denominator. The denominator equals n + a + b + 1, where a + b is the effect of the prior distribution and n is the effect of the data. If a + b is small relative to n, then the prior distribution has very little effect on the posterior distribution. Note that we are talking about the sum a + b, not a and b separately. If n equals 1500 and a + b equals 30, the effect of the prior distribution is minimal, and it makes no difference for the denominator in the posterior variance whether the prior distribution is such that a equals 1 and b equals 29 or whether we have any other pair of values for a and b such that their sum equals 30.

Similar conclusions follow if we look at other formulas. For example, in the analysis of the mean from a normal distribution, the mean of the posterior distribution is arrived at as a weighted combination of the prior mean and the data mean. The weights are the inverses of the corresponding variances, and because the sample size occurs in the denominator of the variance of the sample mean, we find that for large samples the prior distributions typically have little or no effect on the posterior distribution.

These results are examples of what is known as the principle of *stable estimation*, which states that even somewhat informative prior distribution has little or no effect on the posterior distribution in face of large samples. The reason for this is that with data from a large sample, the probability of these data is very close to zero except for a narrow range of values of the parameter(s). For example, equation 14 gives the probability of obtaining 420 Catholics and 1410 non-Catholics in a sample of 1830 respondents. The binomial coefficient in that probability is a constant that gets absorbed in Bayes' theorem, and the important part of the data probability is contained in the remaining expression $\pi^{420}(1 - \pi)^{1410}$, technically known as the likelihood function. For each value of π this gets multiplied by the value of the prior distribution for the same value of π in the numerator of Bayes' theorem. But the expression above is essentially equal to zero for π less than 0.20 and larger than 0.26 and it is very peaked in the interval between those two values. This means that the posterior distribution will be essentially equal to zero for π less than 0.20 and larger than 0.26 regardless of the values of the prior distribution in that range. The effect of the prior distribution is felt only in the interval between 0.20 and 0.26, and most gentle priors would be almost rectangular across such a short interval. Thus the shape of the posterior distribution would be almost completely determined by the shape of the likelihood function, and most of the posterior distribution is found over the interval consisting of the parameter values favored by the data.

Stable estimation accounts for a good deal of the numerical correspondence that exists between Bayesian and classical statistics. It explains why Bayesian probability intervals and classical confidence intervals often coincide numerically, so that we can interpret the confidence intervals as Bayesian intervals. It also explains why it is that when faced with strong evidence from the data, people with different prior distributions will frequently end up with the same posterior distribution.

The converse is also true. When there is only limited information available from the data, meaning we have small samples or large variances or both, then different prior distributions will lead to different posterior distributions. The posterior distributions will not be as different as the prior distributions are, because the prior distributions will all have been modified by the same data. But there may not be enough information in the data to have all the different prior distributions converge to a single posterior distribution.

7. BAYESIAN DIFFICULTIES

Bayes' theorem uses a prior probability distribution and the conditional data probabilities as input to compute the posterior distribution of the parameter(s). Difficulties can arise in all three areas: finding the prior distribution, finding the data probabilities, and manipulating Bayes' theorem in order to find the posterior distribution. In this chapter we take a closer look at each of these three types of difficulties that can occur in Bayesian statistics.

Priors

Finding the proper prior distribution can be difficult. When we have some vague prior knowledge about a parameter, we have to translate this knowledge into a probability distribution. In Chapter 6 we discuss ways in which this can be done, and it can be a difficult process.

In particular, finding an informative prior distribution for a multivariate analysis can become very difficult. A multivariate regression analysis, for example, uses an intercept, a regression coefficient for each variable, and the variance of the residuals. A proper prior distribution of these parameters consists of a multivariate distribution containing all the information we have about each parameter as well as about all the possible interrelations among the parameters. Even with only a few parameters this is hard to do, at best, and with many parameters it is next to impossible to find such a joint distribution.

Most often we resort to rectangular, noninformative, and independent prior distributions in multivariate situations. That way we avoid the difficulty of trying to express the possible prior relationships between the parameters, and the joint posterior distribution basically contains the information about the parameters we obtain from the data.

Data Probabilities

Several instances in Chapter 5 on Bayesian methods make use of the assumption that the data are normally distributed. This enables us to substitute the formula for the normal distribution in Bayes' theorem and thereby derive mathematically the resulting posterior distribution. In the case of a population proportion we assume the data follow the binomial distribution and use the formula for that distribution in Bayes' theorem.

What happens if the data do not follow the particular distribution we use as the data probability in Bayes' theorem? How much is the resulting posterior distribution affected by deviation from the assumed data distribution, and how free are we to use other data probabilities? The sensitivity to deviations from assumed data probabilities is known as the issue of robustness, and it concerns both Bayesian and classical statisticians. Deviation from normality is often studied in terms of skewness and kurtosis, where the normal distribution is symmetric and has no kurtosis, which refers to how heavy the tails of the distribution are.

The Bayesian approach to deviations from normality consists of using a more general data probability than the normal distribution. Such distributions typically have parameters for skewness and kurtosis in addition to parameters for central value and dispersion. With prior distributions for the parameters it is possible to derive posterior distributions for the parameters. This process is considerably more complicated than the methods discussed here, and the reader is referred to Box and Tiao (1973), who discuss certain models for deviations from normality.

For a further discussion of Bayesian robustness see Berger (1980).

Computation

With conjugate prior distributions Bayes' theorem easily produces posterior distributions, and in those situations we do not even see the theorem itself. But with more complicated prior distributions we may have to go back to first principles and use the theorem to derive the posterior distribution.

When the parameter is discrete, as in the example in Chapter 3, we have to compute the posterior probability for each value of the parameter as shown in Table 1. For a continuous parameter it is possible to end up with integrals that have to be handled with numerical methods. With modern computers this is not necessarily difficult; therefore we should not shy away from using prior distributions that do not give mathematically simple posterior distributions.

8. BAYESIAN STRENGTHS

The part of statistics concerned with inference from sample to population has been dominated by classical statistics, particularly hypothesis testing. In this chapter I discuss some strengths of Bayesian inference and why we should change to Bayesian statistical inference in both research and in training of future social scientists.

The reasons for changing to Bayesian statistics fall in two groups: specific and general. The specific reasons arise because there are certain problems that cannot be handled by classical methods, while they present no problems for Bayesian statistics. As pointed out in Chapter 5, the comparison of two means in populations with unequal variances is one example of such a problem. Another example, discussed below, is known as the problem of stopping rules and deals with the study of a population proportion under various sampling plans. The general reasons center around the idea that Bayesian inference is directly tailored to the research process, starting with the initial uncertainty about the parameters and then updating this uncertainty in the face of new information from the data. There is none of the awkwardness of classical statistics with its use of the double negative, in which it is assumed that the complement of the research hypothesis is true and then studying whether the data are inconsistent with this assumption.

Specific Reasons

Different means, unequal variances. One statistical problem that has no exact, classical solution is how to test the null hypothesis that two population means are equal when the corresponding population variances are unequal. Even though the answer is complicated mathematically and it is easier to use the approximate solution shown in Chapter 5, Bayesian statistics does provide a way of studying the difference between the two means.

Stopping rules. How large a role should our intentions play and how large a role should our data play in reaching conclusions from our research? Classical statistics claims that the data should speak for themselves, which means that there is no room for something like prior distributions.

Let us examine the follwing situation, however. The null hypothesis states that 30 percent of the population favor increased military spending. In a random sample of n = 10 people it was found x = 1 person in favor. In line with trends in classical statistics, instead of choosing a significance level and seeing if the null hypothesis is rejected, let us report the one-sided p-value and let the readers themselves decide whether to reject or not. The p-value is the probability of the observed data and any other more extreme data that could have occurred; that is, the smallest significance level for which the null hypothesis would be rejected.

We observed one person in favor, and an even more extreme situation would have been to have nobody in favor. Using the binomial distribution with n = 10 and $\pi = 0.3$, we find that the probabilities of one or zero add up to 0.15—by most standards not small enough to be significant. The classical interpretation of this result is that if we drew many samples of 10 from this population, then 15 percent of these samples would have either 0 or 1 person in favor of increased military spending, assuming the null hypothesis is true.

At this point matters get more complicated because the researcher informs us, "Actually, I wanted to have a sample containing 1 person in favor, and I had to sample as many as 10 people before I found one in favor." In other words, even though we are still dealing with the same data, the researcher intended x = 1 person in favor to be fixed, while the sample size n = 10 is the random quantity. In another sample with one person in favor we might have found a sample of 7 or 11 or some other number. The observed data consist of n = 10, and more extreme data would have been 11 or 12 or anything larger. The probability of each of these possible values of n is found from the negative binomial distribution, and the sum of these probabilities equals the p-value, here 0.05, borderline significant with a one-sided test. The classical interpretation of this probability is that if we draw many samples containing exactly one person in favor, then 5 percent of these samples would have 10 or more observations, assuming the null hypothesis is true.

In the first case the p-value equals 0.15 and in the second case it equals 0.05. Thus, one p-value is as much as three times as large as the other, even though the data are the same in both cases. The data consist of 1 person in favor and 9 not in favor; the only difference is that in the first case we intended to take 10 observations and count how many were in favor, while in the second case we intended to keep on sampling until we found one person in favor.

Even more complications arise when the researchers tell us they simply collected some data and ended up with 10 people, one of whom was in favor. There was no plan to collect 10 observations nor keep sampling until 1 person was found to be in favor. It just happened that those were the data when the sampling stopped. In this case classical statistics has nothing to offer for the analysis of these data. Without knowledge of the researchers' intention about how the data were to be collected, no formal model can be used in the statistical analysis and no analysis is possible.

Bayesian inference does not care whether the data collection stopped after ten observations, after the first person in favor, or for some other reason. All that matters are the data themselves. The information in the data consists of 1 person in favor and 9 people not in favor, and this information is expressed mathematically in the likelihood function $\pi^1(1 - \pi)^9$ for this example and $\pi^x(1 - \pi)^{n-x}$ in the general case. The likelihood function is combined with the prior distribution, and if the prior is a beta distribution, then we know from Chapter 4 that the posterior distribution is also the beta distribution no matter why we stopped collecting data.

General Reasons

One advantage of Bayesian over classical statistical inference is the cumulative feature of Bayesian statistics. The fact that we can express our prior opinion of a parameter in a prior distribution means that we do not have to start at the very beginning again each time. There are many times when we do have prior information, and that makes it possible to use informative prior distributions. With informative prior distributions we get posterior distributions that are more peaked and with smaller variances. This means we can assess the unknown parameters with more precision and therefore get shorter Bayesian probability intervals for the parameters than we do with noninformative prior distributions.

One example in which prior information may be available occurs when data are collected over time. The General Social Survey at the University of Chicago and the American election studies at the University of Michigan now go back decades, and each study gives us information that can be used in the analysis of the following study. Even though questions are repeated in order to allow for the study of change over time, the previous studies contain a wealth of information that can be used for our prior distributions.

Another advantage of Bayesian statistics is a pedagogical one. Most social scientists have only limited training in statistics. A typical graduate program in one of the social sciences contains two or three courses in statistics, and most undergraduate programs have fewer. Much material is covered, and litle time is available for statistical inference. Particularly for people with limited mathematical aptitude, concepts like significance level, power of a test, sampling distribution, and confidence interval have been difficult to understand.

With its more general notion of uncertainty, Bayesian inference is more natural and the conclusions much easier to understand. Not only students but even authors of textbooks in statistics for social science students have difficulties with a concept like a confidence interval. Similar difficulties do not seem to be present when it comes to learning about Bayesian probability intervals.

This point becomes even more pronounced when people with no formal training in statistics have to make use of statistical results in their work. This situation occurs, for instance, when a statistical consultant is employed as an expert—say, in a courtroom where jurors, lawyers, and judges have to understand the results of the statistician's work. Kaye (1982) discusses five possible statistical analyses of the same data: presentation of a p-value, rejection of a null hypothesis, display of a prediction interval, presentation of the likelihood function, and Bayesian treatment. He gets sidetracked into a discussion of problems with the prior distribution and does not particularly recommend the Bayesian alternative. But my own experience in similar situations has shown the strong pedagogical advantages of the Bayesian point of view.

Finally, the reason Bayesian inference is so much more natural is that it is more closely geared to the research process itself than is classical inference. The research problem starts with an initial uncertainty about one or more parameters, data are collected in order to increase our information about the parameters, and in light of the new information, the initial uncertainty has been reduced.

This description of research is also a description of Bayesian statistical inference. It starts with a prior distribution of the parameters, computes the probability of the data given various parameter values, and combines the prior distribution with the data probabilities using Bayes' theorem, and the end result is a posterior distribution of the parameters. Bayesian inference uses the concept of probability to express uncertainty about the quantities of which we are truly uncertain, namely the unknown parameters. Classical inference, on the other hand, computes the probability of the observed data. But there is nothing uncertain about the observed data. They are known and are there for everyone to see.

When a null hypothesis is rejected in classical statistics, how many of us have thought, "That probably means the null hypothesis is false, even though we cannot be quite certain?" Whether we know it or not, we slip into a Bayesian way of interpretation even though we think we are doing classical statistical inference. Classical statistics, however, does not permit statements like the one above. The null hypothesis is either true or not, for certain; only, we do not know whether it is true or not. The quotation above implies that the particular null hypothesis is true some of the time and not true other times, since probability is defined as a relative frequency.

Instead of slipping into Bayesian interpretations such as that, we should be honest with ourselves by taking the consequences of this way of thinking and do the entire analysis the Bayesian way. We should admit we are uncertain about the parameters; from this it follows that the way to deal with such uncertainty is through Bayesian statistical inference.

REFERENCES

BARNETT, V. (1982) Comparative Statistical Inference. New York: John Wiley.

BAYES, T. (1763) "Essay towards solving a problem in the doctrine of chances." Philosophical Transactions. Royal Society, London 53: 370-418. (Reprinted in Biometrika, 1958, 45: 293-315.)

BERGER, J. (1980) Statistical Decision Theory: Foundations, Concepts and Methods. New York: Springer-Verlag.

BERNARDO, J. M., M. H. DeGROOT, D. V. LINDLEY, and A.F.M. SMITH [eds.] (1980) Bayesian Statistics. Proceedings of the First International Meeting, Valencia, Spain. Valencia, Spain: University Press.

BOX, G.E.P. and G. C. TIAO (1973) Bayesian Inference in Statistical Analysis. Reading, MA: Addison-Wesley.

CAMPBELL, A. and P. E. CONVERSE (1980) Quality of American Life, 1978. Conducted by the Institute for Social Research, University of Michigan, ICPSR ed. Ann Arbor, MI: Inter-university Consortium for Political and Social Research. (machine readable data file)

DeFINNETTI, B. (1982) "Probability and my life," in J. Gani (ed.) The Making of Statisticians. New York: Springer-Verlag.

EDWARDS, W., H. LINDMAN, and L. J. SAVAGE (1963) "Bayesian statistical inference for psychological research." Psychological Review 70 (May): 193-242.

ELDER, G. H., Jr. (1969) "Appearance and education in marriage mobility." American Sociological Review 34: 524.

HENKEL, R. E. (1976) Tests of Significance. Beverly Hills, CA: Sage.

IVERSEN, G. R. and H. NORPOTH (1976) Analysis of Variance. Beverly Hills, CA: Sage.

JEFFREY, R. C. (1983) The Logic of Decision. Chicago: University of Chicago Press.

JEFFREYS, H. (1961) Theory of Probability. Oxford: Clarendon Press.

KAYE, D. (1982) "Statistical evidence of discrimination." Journal of the American Statistical Association 77 (December): 773-783.

KYBURG, H. E., Jr. and H. E. SMOKLER [eds.] (1980) Studies in Subjective Probability. Huntington, NY: R. E. Kreiger.

LINDLEY, D. V. (1965) Introduction to Probability and Statistics from a Bayesian Viewpoint (2 vols.). Cambridge: Cambridge University Press.

PHILLIPS, L. D. (1974) Bayesian Statistics for Social Scientists. New York: Crowell.

RAIFFA, H. (1968) Decision Analysis. Reading, MA: Addison-Wesley.

RAMSEY, F. P. (1926) "Truth and probability," in The Foundation of Mathematics and Other Logical Essays. London: Routledge & Kegan Paul. (Reprinted in Kyberg and Smokler [1964].)

ROSENKRANTZ, R. D. (1977) Inference, Method and Decision. Towards a Bayesian Philosophy of Science. Dordrecht, Holland: D. Reidel.

SAVAGE, L. J. (1954) The Foundations of Statistics. New York: John Wiley.

SCHMITT, S. A. (1969) Measuring Uncertainty. An Elementary Introduction to Bayesian Statistics. Reading, MA: Addison-Wesley.

VENN, J. (1886) The Logic of Chance. London: MacMillan. (Reprinted by Chelsea, New York, 1963.)

GUDMUND R. IVERSEN is Professor of Statistics and directs the Center for Social and Policy Studies at Swarthmore College. He has published on the application of statistics to the social sciences, including a statistics textbook and a co-authored book on contextual analysis. As a graduate student he worked for a year for Jimmy Savage, and during that time he was converted to Bayesianism. He holds master's degrees in mathematics and sociology from the University of Michigan and a Ph. D. in statistics from Harvard University. Dr. Iversen is co-author of the first volume in this series, Analysis of Variance *[1976].*